ISLAM EXPOSED

WHAT YOU NEED TO KNOW ABOUT THE WORLD'S MOST DANGEROUS RELIGION

LAWRENCE PAUL HEBRON

ISBN-13: 9781522777946
ISBN-10: 1522777946
Library of Congress Control Number: 2015920856
CreateSpace Independent Publishing Platform
North Charleston, South Carolina

THIS BOOK IS DEDICATED TO GOD,

THE UNITED STATES OF AMERICA,

*AND THE HUNDREDS OF MILLIONS OF
VICTIMS OF ISLAM —*

PAST AND PRESENT.

THIS BOOK IS COMMITTED TO ENSURE

THAT THERE WILL BE NO MORE VICTIMS.

TABLE OF CONTENTS

PART ONE

GETTING STARTED

CHAPTER ONE

INTRODUCTION

I had just completed a portion of my morning run when I heard someone call, "Mr. Hebron!" I looked around to see one of my former students. I trotted over, greeted him, and began to catch up on what he had been doing since the last time I saw him. It wasn't long before his mother came out and greeted me as well. In the truest and best maternal fashion, she began bragging (quite deservedly) about her son's many scholastic and athletic accomplishments. I'm sure I was almost as proud as she was. She then asked what I had been doing. Among other things, I mentioned that I was writing a primer on Islam. She was quick to interject that her older daughter was taking a class on Islam at one the most prestigious Bible colleges in Southern California where she was enrolled. So far, our conversation had been a delightful and welcomed diversion from my run, but what Mom said next changed all that. She announced that her daughter had learned that Muhammad "was really a man of peace, and that it was his followers who had perverted his teachings and made Islam violent." She had a look of confidence and satisfaction on her face, as though she had just passed on a valuable gem of knowledge and wisdom. Although I could not see it, I imagine that my expression must have been quite different. The implications of her brief statement hit me like a punch to the gut.

Teetering between shock and disgust, I asked, "Is that what they're teaching your daughter?"

A hint of bewilderment painted her features as though she could tell from my words and my tone that something was wrong. "Well, yes," she replied hesitantly.

I proceeded to give them both a very short class on the life of this "man of peace." The eyes of Mom and Son slowly widened as they beheld the horror. As we parted, I, too, considered the horror — but of a different kind. It doesn't surprise me that institutions of "higher education" (or is it "greater degradation") purvey pro-Islamic propaganda after receiving millions of dollars from Saudi Arabia (usually) to establish "Islamic Study" programs. This kind of academic prostitution is contemptible, but all too common. But when I hear that Christian institutions are also doing the work of the Jihadists, I cannot feel very optimistic about the future.

The vast majority of Americans are very ignorant about Islam, and what they think they know is superficial and, frankly, often inaccurate. For many, Islam is that "other religion" that really isn't all that different from "our religion." We call God "Jehovah," they call him "Allah." Our

Savior is Jesus, theirs is Muhammad. Our holy book is called the *Bible*, theirs is the *Koran* — which bears many similarities to ours. After all, their Suras, or chapters, begin, "In the Name of God, the Merciful, the Compassionate." That sounds a lot like us. And the *Koran* mentions Adam and Noah and Abraham and Isaac and Ishmael and Lot and Moses and Jonah and David and Solomon and Elisha and Mary and Jesus. It even calls Jesus, "Messiah!" We really aren't all that different, are we? Can't we all just get along? Like the bumper sticker says, "COEXIST."

Yes, the vast majority of Americans are very ignorant about Islam, and would be happy to keep it that way. But then, Islam literally exploded onto the pages of our newspapers, the covers of our magazines, and the screens of our televisions. We heard about such things as Hamas, Hezbollah, the Islamic Brotherhood, Al Qaeda, Taliban, Boko Haram, Tehran, Baghdad, Benghazi, Libya, Iran, Iraq, Afghanistan, ayatollahs, mullas, imams, Khomeini, Qaddafi, bin Laden, Ahmadinejad, Khameini, the Beirut Barracks, Pan Am Flight 103, the USS Cole, suicide bombers, beheadings, Charlie Hebdo, the Paris massacre, 911, ISIS/ISIL, and now my own hometown, San Bernardino. We heard these things, and we began to wonder if we were paying a grave price for our ignorance. Perhaps "COEXIST" was not an option.

But, maybe that's unfair, if not a bit hysterical. Aren't these people and these events which are covered by our media just examples of a radical and unrepresentative minority of Muslims? Most Muslims are moderate, good people who just want to live in peace like the rest of us. Right?

Well, either they are or they aren't; and how we resolve that issue just may decide whether we live or die — whether we commit a terrible injustice, or become the victim of one.

It is not the intent of this book to give a comprehensive account of Islamic theology and history — although, certainly, the book discusses elements of both. The mission of this book is to give the reader a starter course on Islam — to familiarize you with some basic information which you need to know in order to make informed decisions. One of the "traditionists" of Islam, Abu Huraira warned, "Do not accept anything save the Hadiths of the Prophet" (Bukhari, 1:98). The hadiths are narratives about the life and sayings of Muhammad. I urge you to follow that advice. Consider carefully exactly what Muhammad said and did. Then, and only then, will you know the heart and intentions of Islam.

In the pages to follow, the reader will learn the truth about Islam taken from its own words. The vast majority of the facts presented in this text come from the three authoritative and authorized sources of Islam itself: the *Koran*, the *Sirat Rasul Allah* or *Sira* (*The Life of Allah's Messenger* — an authorized biography), and the *Hadith* by Bukhari and others (a collection of narratives or "traditions" about Muhammad, his life, his beliefs, and his associates). In short, you will learn about Islam from the Islamists, although many of these truths were not intended for public consumption by the non-believers. As you will learn, there is a deliberate campaign to keep you in the dark about many things until it is too late to protect yourself from them.

Documentation for quoted material will be placed in parentheses immediately after the quotation. This is not only to show the reader the source of the quotation, but also to help him keep from losing his place should he want to check the source. You won't have to look for footnotes at the bottom of the page, the end of the chapter, or the back of the book. For example, (*Sira*, 153) refers to section 153 of *Sirat Rassul Allah*. (Bukhari, 1:98) refers to hadith number 98 in volume one of Bukhari's collection of hadiths. (*Koran*, 9:5) refers to the fifth verse of Sura Number 9 in the *Koran*. Unfortunately, the numbering of verses is not consistent throughout all translations of the *Koran*. So, if the reader would like to confirm a quoted verse from the *Koran* and does not find it where I indicated it would be, search a few verses before or after my notation, and you should find it.

Occasionally, you will see parenthetic notations (fancy talk for "words in parentheses" — like the ones surrounding this remark) within a quote. These are part of the quoted text and **not** my comments. Islamic traditionists often added editorial comments to enhance clarity. Any comments which I add for elaboration or clarification within a quote or elsewhere will be placed within brackets — [like these].

One more administrative note before we begin. As you will see, the second chapter in this book is the glossary. This is not conventional, but I hope it will be helpful to the reader. DO NOT SKIP IT. Glossaries are usually discovered as an appendix at the back of books after the reader has been thoroughly bewildered by the use of unfamiliar terms in the main text of the book. Your understanding of the material to follow will be much easier if you start with a working understanding of the terms in the glossary. In fact, just reading the glossary alone will provide a reasonably good short course on Islam.

A final note before we begin. Many teachers, advocates, activists, protagonists, etc., write and talk about how important it is to educate the people. Good for them. Frankly, I don't want to educate you. I want to inspire you to act. Education is a good start, but it is a horrible finish. Unless you do something with what you learn, your education is pointless. Accordingly, at the end of this book are some recommendations on how to use the education you will receive by reading this book. These recommendations will most definitely not be the kinds of things you usually hear from the politicians, diplomats, scholars, pastors, and other noise-makers who have dominated the scene for decades and accomplished nothing but the wastage of oceans of blood, thousands of lives, and trillions of dollars. I am not interested in "kicking the can down the road." I am interested in solving the problem; and when the problem is as grave and intractable as Islam, I'm afraid that speeches, negotiations, lectures, sermons, and other unavailing claptrap serve no productive purpose. I know my recommendations will be spurned by many and dismissed as bellicose ravings — for now. The same was true of Winston Churchill in the early 1930s as he warned of the dangers of Nazism and pronounced the need to stand firm against its aggression. The Chamberlains and Quislings of the modern era will urge appeasement, conciliation, and compromise, just as they did in the past. Listening to them today will have the same — or worse — results as it did in the past. Unless we learn from history and then apply its lessons, we will end up no better than those victims whom we study.

CHAPTER TWO

GLOSSARY OF TERMS

Allah. The term used by Muslims for "god." It derives from the Arabic "al-ilah," which translates as "the god." Pre-Muhammad Arabians recognized hundreds of gods. The use of the term "Allah" pre-dates Islam. This pre-Islamic use of the term meant "the god" as well, but also referred to a moon god known as "Ilah." Muslims do not worship a moon god, but lunar imagery is commonplace in Islam. Lunar cycles are important for determining dates, and the crescent moon is a worldwide symbol of Islam.

Ablution. The act of ritual washing prior to performing prayers and other religious rituals.

Abrogation. This concept is presented in verse 2:106 of the *Koran*. It states that if two verses in the *Koran* contradict each other, the more recent one abrogates, or cancels, the older. Generally speaking, nearly all the peaceful references in the *Koran* were written during an early period and are abrogated by more recent verses, such as the "Verse of the Sword," *Koran*, 9:5.

Caliph. A totalitarian Islamic leader whose power and influence equates to a combination of king, pope, and generalissimo.

Dhimmi / Dhimmitude. "Dhimma" means compact or contract. A "Dhimmi" is a term used to refer to a "protected person" (protected by the terms of a "contract") within an Islamic nation or community. A Dhimmi is a person who chooses not to accept Islam. Unlike many non-believers who are killed or enslaved, a Dhimmi may live within the Islamic community, but they pay a considerable price. They have no civil rights, cannot worship or show any signs of their faith in public, cannot testify in courts against a Muslim, and must pay a poll tax, or "jizya" that can be as high as 50% of their total income. "Dhimmitude" is the institution or practice which incorporates the Dhimmi into the Islamic society. Dhimmitude is a tactic for wearing down opponents while deriving a financial benefit from them.

Hadith. The word "hadith" means "report," "account," or "narrative." In an Islamic context, it usually refers to a short account or story about something Muhammad did or said. Hundreds of thousands of them exist, although some are considered apocryphal. The most respected collections of hadiths come from Muhammad al-Bukhari and Muslim ibn al-Hajjaj. Collectively, they are known as the Hadith ("Accounts" or "Traditions"), and comprise part of the Trilogy of Islamic authoritative texts: the *Koran*, the *Sirat Rasul Allah* (the authorized biography of Muhammad, also known as the *Sira*), and the *Hadith*. Although most non-believers are familiar with the *Koran*, it represents less than 20% of the total verbiage in the Trilogy. Most of the instructions for living an Islamic life and much of the basis for Sharia Law come from the *Sira* and the *Hadith*. In this book, you will see parenthetic notations following quotes such as (Bukhari, 1:98). This means that the quote came from Hadith number 98 in Volume One of the narratives (hadith) assembled by Bukhari. Also, "ahadith" is the correct, plural form of the word "hadith" in Arabic, but I will use the more conventional means of pluralizing for English-speakers by simply adding an "s."

Islam. The word "Islam" means "submission" or "surrender." Islam is not merely a religion. It is a comprehensive lifestyle encompassing religious, political, and cultural elements. As a religion, it is a monotheistic faith based on 114 revelations allegedly transmitted by Allah (the god) through the angel Gabriel to the last and greatest prophet, Muhammad, and collected in the *Koran*. The religion is "works" based and promises Paradise to believers and Hell to non-believers. As a political system, it emphasizes the eventual conquest, subjugation, and annihilation of non-Islamic peoples and cultures. As a culture, it dictates many elements of day-to-day life including various customs affecting such areas as clothing, food, entertainment, etc. The life of Muhammad presents the sacred pattern for the perfect life; and since both Allah and Muhammad hate non-believers as long as they remain non-believers, anything can be done to them with the goal of converting them or destroying them.

Kaaba. The word "Kaaba" (also spelled Kaba, Kabah, and others) drives from the Arabic word for "the cube" or the "square house." It is a cubical building at the center of Islam's most sacred mosque, Al-Masjid al-Haram, in Mecca, Saudi Arabia. Its height is reported to be between 39.5 and 43 feet. Its sides measure roughly 36 feet by 42 feet. The history of the Kaaba precedes the founding of Islam. Muhammad claimed that it was initially constructed by Abraham and his son Ishmael. It is reputed to be the burial site of Ishmael and his mother, Hagar. Muslims are expected to make a pilgrimage, or "Hajj," to Mecca at least once in their lifetime. During that Hajj, they will take part in "tawaf" wherein they walk around the Kaaba seven times in a counter-clockwise direction.

Kafir. The word "Kafir" comes from a root word that means "deny." Accordingly, a "Kafir" is one who "denies" Islam. The word is usually translated as "non-believer," or "infidel." Actually, it has a strong pejorative connotation and equates to a vile slur referring to non-Muslims.

Koran / Qur'an. The word "Koran" means "recitation." This sacred text of the Islamic religion is claimed to be a collection of divine revelations provided by Allah (the god) to Muhammad through the angel Gabriel. "This *Koran* could not have been forged apart from God…" (*Koran*, 10:37). These revelations are organized into 114 "suras" or "chapters." It is the best-known of the Trilogy of authoritative texts of Islam, but it provides the least actual guidance of the three for living the Muslim life. Only roughly one third of the *Koran* deals with how to live properly as a Muslim. The remaining two-thirds is devoted to dealings with Kafirs and the telling of various tales. The other two texts of the Islamic Trilogy are the *Sirat Rasul Allah*, or *Sira* (the authorized biography of Muhammad) and the "Hadith" or collection of traditions regarding the life of Muhammad. Since Muhammad is alleged to have lived a perfect life, his words and actions are the true guide for Muslims, and most of these are recorded in the *Sira* and *Hadith*, not the *Koran*. The *Koran* is considered by my Muslims to be perfect, universal, complete, and final.

Some scholars refer to "two *Korans*" — the Meccan and the Medinan. There really is only one *Koran,* but the nature of the suras written while Muhammad was in Mecca is very different from those written later when Muhammad and his Muslims had migrated to Medina. Most of the suras were written by Muhammad during his initial, Meccan period — the roughly thirteen years that Muhammad tried to establish his religion in his home town of Mecca. These are the more "religious" suras, but their basic message boils down to this: worship Allah and accept Muhammad as his last and greatest prophet or you will suffer a "great chastisement" in Hell after your death. Muhammad also passed along many stories from the Old Testament, although with self serving modifications that would have been unrecognizable to most Jews. He could get away with this in Mecca where there were very few Jews to contradict him.

Things changed after Muhammad's move to Medina, and the nature of the suras also changed to support Muhammad's evolution into a warlord. The message became more bellicose and violent, jihad and dhimmitude were introduced, and the punishment for Kafirs for their infidelity would begin here on earth and not wait until after their death. Most of the "nice" and "peaceful" verses quoted by the Islamic apologists to support their claim that Islam is a peaceful religion are found in the suras written during the earlier, Meccan period. They would be "abrogated," or cancelled out, by the more recent, Medinan verses.

Inconveniently for Muhammad, there also were many more Jews living in and around Medina than lived in Mecca, and they called him on the unscriptural changes he had made to many of their traditional stories. Muhammad did not take kindly to this, and we see the Jews treated much more harshly in the Medinan suras.

Mecca. Located in modern-day Saudi Arabia, Mecca is the birthplace of Muhammad, the spiritual capital of Islam, and the location of the Kaaba — a cubical building regarded as the most sacred site in Islam and the physical object of the pilgrimage, or Hajj, that every Muslim is expected to take at least once in his lifetime.

Medina. Known as the "Radiant City," Medina is located in modern-day Saudi Arabia about 210 miles northwest from Mecca. Following his failed attempts to build Islam in Mecca, Muhammad and about 150 followers moved to Medina. It is here that his approach became more militant, and Islam began to spread by the sword. Medina served as the effective capital of a rapidly growing Islamic Empire, initially under Muhammad, and then under the first three caliphs (religious / political leaders): Abu Bakr, Umar, and Uthman.

Muhammad. Muhammad was born around the year 570 AD in the town of Mecca and died June 8, 632. He founded Islam after claiming to receive divine revelations from Allah through the angel Gabriel. Although initially unsuccessful as a religious leader, Muhammad prevailed as a warlord whose political and religious system was advanced by the sword. Muhammad is the model Muslim. The *Koran* states more than seventy times that every human should live his life by following the example of Muhammad. Accordingly, whatever Muhammad did is considered acceptable, even required, by other Muslims.

Moslem / Muslim. Due to differences in transliteration (the process of converting a word in one language into a different language with a different alphabet), both the words "Moslem" and "Muslim" can refer to adherents of Islam. According to the *Hadith* of Bukhari, 1:6, "Muslims" are "those who have surrendered to Allah." However, the Arabic roots of the two words reveal that they are very different. Whereas "Muslim" refers to one who has surrendered to god, "Moslem" (pronounced "Mozlem") means "one who is evil and unjust."

Sharia Law. Sharia is the Islamic legal system. The word "sharia" means "road." Sharia law offers a pathway for institutionalizing the tenets of Islam in a society. It offers a religious and moral code reputedly derived from divine revelation and not human jurisprudence. The specific elements of this legal system are taken from the authoritative trilogy of Islamic writings: the *Sira*, the *Hadith*, and the *Koran*. Since Sharia Law is believed by Muslims to be divinely inspired, it is absolute, inflexible, incontrovertible, and unchangeable.

Shia. Shia Muslims, or Shias, make up Islam's second largest denomination. They represent about 12% of the total number of Muslims. The term "shia" refers to the "followers" of Muhammad's son-in-law and cousin, Ali. Shias consider Ali to have been the divinely appointed successor to Muhammad and the first true caliph, not the fourth as held by the Sunnis. Although the Shias and Sunnis hold some differing views in religion, politics, and who may serve as caliph, they generally are united in their relentless opposition to the non-Muslim world, or Kafirs.

Sira. The word "Sira" refers to "the life" or "the way" but also can be used to mean "biography." A reference to "the Sira" when speaking of the life of Muhammad is often an allusion to the authorized biography of Muhammad, compiled by Muhammad Ibn Ishaq. Its full title in the Arabic is *Sirat Rasul Allah*, meaning *"The Life of Allah's Messenger" or "The Life of the Messenger of God."* The *Sira* along with the *Koran* and the *Hadith* constitute the trilogy of authoritative writings of Islam.

Sunnah / Sunna. The word "Sunnah" is derived from an Arabic expression referring to a clear, well-traveled path. For Muslims, the Sunnah is a righteous lifestyle based upon the teachings, practices, habits, and values of Muhammad. Muhammad is the exemplar which Muslims are expected to emulate. Therefore, the Sunnah encompasses all the elements of leading a godly life.

Sunni. Sunni Muslims constitute the largest sect or denomination within Islam. They represent about 85% of the total number of Muslims. The name derives from the Arabic word, "Sunnah" (a clear, well-traveled path), and Sunnis are considered "people of the way." By far the largest sect within Islam, Sunnis are the largest religious denomination in the world and the second largest religious body, following Christians.

Sura / Surah. A "sura" is a chapter in the *Koran*. There are 114 chapters in the *Koran*. Eighty-six of these chapters are considered to be Meccan and twenty-eight are Medinan, depending on whether the alleged revelations to Muhammad happened during the time he was residing in Mecca or Medina. They are not organized chronologically, but generally by length, starting with the longest and ending with the shortest.

PART TWO

MUHAMMAD

"Allah has said, 'Verily, in Allah's Apostle you have a good example."
(Bukhari, 2:693)

"Every Prophet was sent to his nation but only I have been sent to all mankind."
(Bukhari, 1:7,331)

CHAPTER THREE

THE MESSIAH OF MECCA

If you want to understand Islam, do not study the *Koran;* study the life of Muhammad. Islam is Muhammad, and Muhammad is Islam. Whatever he said is "sacred." Whatever he did is permissible — in fact, required. He is the exemplar — the model Muslim who must be emulated. The *Koran* itself asserts this over seventy times.

The three authoritative sources of documentation for Islam — its Trilogy — are the *Koran*, written down by Muhammad; the *Sirat Rasul Allah*, or *Sira*, a biography of Muhammad compiled by Muhammad ibn Ishaq, and the *Hadith*, a vast collection of narratives and traditions based largely on the sayings and actions of Muhammad. As you can see, it's all about Muhammad. Faithful followers might retort, "No, it's all about submission to the will of Allah!" Yes, but everything a Muslim knows about the will of Allah came from a single source: Muhammad. Know him, and you know Islam. Obey Muhammad, and you obey Allah. In fact, Muhammad said exactly this: "He who obeys me, obeys

23

Allah, and he who disobeys me, disobeys Allah" (Bukhari, 4:204). If you want to understand Islam, get to know Muhammad. If you want to anticipate what the Islamic world is up to, get to know Muhammad. Let's do that.

Muhammad's full name is Abū al-Qāsim Muḥammad ibn ʿAbd Allāh ibn ʿAbd al-Muṭṭalib ibn Hāshim. "Muhammad" means "praiseworthy." He was born on a Monday, the twelfth day of Rabi ul-Awwal (or Rabīʿ al-Awwal) in the Year of the Elephant — which would put it around the year 570 AD — in the town of Mecca. He died June 8, 632. Muhammad's father, Abdullah (which means "slave of Allah") died while Muhammad's mother was pregnant. His mother died when he was six. Muhammad's grandfather assumed responsibility for his upbringing, but he died when Muhammad was eight. Thereafter, Muhammad was raised by his uncle, Abu Talib. His uncle was a merchant who traded with businessmen operating in other areas, especially to the north in Syria. Abu Talib and Muhammad were both members of the influential Quraysh tribe. The "Quraysh," or "Quraish," was a powerful clan of merchants that controlled Mecca and the Kaaba. They were reputed to have descended from Ishmael. "For Quraysh were the leaders and guides of men, the people of the sacred temple, and the pure stock of Ishmael son of Abraham..." (*Sira*, 933). Muhammad was born into one of the clans of this tribe. Many of them would later oppose and persecute Muhammad and his followers. They subsequently became a target of Muhammad's wrath.

Muhammad learned from his uncle and soon became a savvy businessman, himself. As a young adult, Muhammad was hired by the widow of a distant cousin to manage her business dealings with merchants in Syria. Her name was Khadija. This brought him into contact with the large Christian and Jewish communities which lived there.

Muhammad had an affinity for spiritual matters. He was already well-versed in the religious views of his native Arabia, where over three hundred religions were practiced. At the time, Arabia was very tolerant of diverse religious views. His exposure to Judeo-Christian tenets would add to the spiritual potpourri brewing in his heart and head and would add a distinctive flavor to the religion he would soon unleash upon the world: Islam.

Muslims consider it sacrilegious to make likenesses of Muhammad, but we do have a description of his physical appearance, which gives an idea of how he looked. It is found in an account by Ibn Hisham. "The following description of the apostle comes from Umar, freedman of Ghufra from Ibrahim b. Muhammad b. Ali b. Abu Talib. 'Ali used to say when he described the apostle: 'He was neither too tall nor unduly short but of normal height; his hair was not too curly nor lank, but definitely curly; his face was not fat nor rounded; it was white tinged with red; his eyes were black, fringed with long lashes; he was firmly knit and broad shouldered; the hair on his body was fine, thick on hands and feet. When he walked he picked his feet up smartly as though he were going down hill, when he turned he turned his whole body; between his shoulders was the seal of prophecy, he being the seal of the prophets"" (Ibn Hisham, 221). This last comment was a reference to some kind of irregular marking on Muhammad's back, perhaps from a birthmark or scar.

Muhammad began taking religious retreats to meditate and study the religious practices of his homeland. In particular, he made a practice of spending several weeks each year alone praying in a cave on Mount Hira. During one of these retreats in 610 at the age of about forty, he claimed to have had a vision in which an angel appeared to him, "and suddenly the Truth descended upon him while he was in the cave of Hira" (Bukhari, 1:3). It was not immediately obvious to Muhammad, however, that what had just happened was a good thing. He initially feared that he was going mad and decided to commit suicide when the angel stopped him, saying, "O Muhammad, you are the apostle of Allah, and I am Gabriel" (*Sira*, 153). "The apostle began to receive revelations in the month of Ramadan. In the words of God, 'The month of Ramadan in which the Quran was brought down as a guidance to men, and proofs of guidance and a decisive criterion'" (*Sira*, 155). From that time on, Muhammad taught lessons which he said Gabriel had revealed to him.

The Islamic faith holds that Allah sent Muhammad "as an apostle. 'To give those who believe, who do good works, the good news that they will have a glorious reward, enjoying it everlastingly,' i.e. the eternal abode. 'They shall not die therein,' i.e. those who have accepted your (Muhammad's) message as true, though others have denied it, and have done the works that you have ordered them to do'" (*Sira*, 193).

At first, Muhammad only shared his message with close family and friends. His first convert was Khadija, his former employer whom he had married and with whom he had six children — two boys who died in childhood, and four girls who lived to be adults. "Khadija believed in him and accepted as true what he brought from God, and helped him in his work. She was the first to believe in God and His apostle, and in the truth of his message" (*Sira*, 155). "Ali was the first male to believe in the apostle of God, to pray with him and to believe in his divine message, when he was a boy of ten" (*Slra*, 159). After Muhammad's death, Ali became a caliph — basically a leader of church and state.

Initially, Muhammad only shared his beliefs among a small circle of acquaintances. "Then God commanded His apostle to declare the truth of what he had received and to make known His commands to men and to call them to Him. Three years elapsed from the time that the apostle concealed his state until God commanded him to publish his religion..." (*Sira*, 166).

It was when Muhammad began his public ministry that the trouble began. The people of Mecca were relatively tolerant of various religious beliefs and practices. We are told that when Muhammad made his triumphal return to Mecca after years in exile at Medina, "there were three hundred-and-sixty idols around the Ka'ba" (Bukhari, 3:658).

The people of Mecca were willing to tolerate another religion, but Muhammad and his religion were not willing to tolerate them. He said that Islam was the only true religion, condemned to Hell those who disagreed, and cursed their gods. As one outraged Meccan put it, Muhammad "has cursed our gods, insulted our religion, mocked our way of life, and accused our forefathers of error…" (*Sira*, 167).

Muhammed also set himself up as the true messenger of Allah whose word must be obeyed as though it were Allah's himself — because, according to Muhammad, it was. The following verses are taken from a single Sura of the *Koran*, the chapter entitled "The Light":

* "We believe in God and the Messenger [Muhammed], and we obey" (24:47).
* "Whoso obeys God and His Messenger, and fears God and has awe of Him, those — they are the triumphant" (24:51).
* "Obey God, and obey the Messenger…" (24:52).
* "It is only for the Messenger to deliver the manifest Message" (24:54).
* "Perform the prayer, and pay the alms, and obey the Messenger …" (24:56).
* "Those only are believers, who believe in God and His Messenger… (24:62).

As you can see, Muhammad set himself up as the sole, living spokesperson for god. He would tolerate no dispute.

Muhammad continued to provoke a great deal of turmoil in Mecca. Eventually, community leaders approached him to seek a reconciliation, but Muhammad told them that they were the ones who needed to be reconciled with Allah by submitting completely to Islam — namely, by following Muhammad's teachings. The Meccan leaders seemed willing to entertain the notion that Muhammad might be correct, but they needed more proof than merely his own endorsement of himself. If Muhammad's god really was the supreme, all-powerful, and singular god, he could prove it by performing a miracle. They suggested that Muhammad ask Allah, "to remove for us these mountains which shut us in, and to straighten out our country for us, and to open up in it rivers like those of Syria and Iraq, and to resurrect for us our forefathers…Ask God to send an angel with him (Muhammad) to confirm what he said…so they would recognize his merit and position with God, if he were an apostle as he claimed to be" (*Sira*, 188-189). Muhammad replied that he was merely a messenger and couldn't tell god what to do. His opponents then cleverly retorted, "Did not your Lord know that we would sit with you, and ask you these questions, so that He might come to you and instruct you how to answer us, and tell you what He was going to do with us, if we did not receive your message?" (*Sira*, 189). They then accused Muhammad of merely repeating stories that others had told before him while positioning himself as the ultimate and unchallengeable spokesperson of god. Muhammad, unable to convince his adversaries with reason, spiritual acumen, or miracles, "got up and left them" (Sira, 189). His position was that, "He had conveyed to them God's message, and they could either accept it with advantage, or reject it and await God's Judgement" (*Sira*, 189).

Powerful groups in Mecca began to persecute the followers of Muhammad. "[E]very clan which contained Muslims [were] attacked [by] them [i.e., the Quraysh], imprisoning them, and beating them, allowing them no food or drink, and exposing them to the burning heat of Mecca, so as to seduce them from their religion" (*Sira*, 205). In the face of this persecution, Muhammad dispatched some of his followers to Abyssinia, trusting its king to protect them (*Sira*, 208). Muhammad, himself, was somewhat shielded from the abuse heaped upon his followers thanks to the protection of his powerful uncle, Abu Talib. But then, "Khadija and Abu Talib died in the same year" and Muhammad's enemies in Mecca "began to treat him in an offensive way which they would not have dared to follow in his uncle's lifetime" (*Sira*, 277). The abuse and danger grew greater, and three years later, in 622, Muhammad joined the other Muslims who had fled to Medina, about 210 miles northwest from Mecca. "The apostle on that day was fifty-three years of age, that being thirteen years after God called him" (*Sira*, 415).

CHAPTER FOUR

THE WARLORD OF MEDINA

The exile in Medina proved to be a critical transition for Muhammad and Islam in many ways. It gave the persecuted sect a chance to survive, recover, and regroup. Furthermore, a model for its political administration was established. "When the apostle was firmly settled in Medina and his brethren[,] the emigrants[,] were gathered to him and the affairs of the helpers were arranged[,] Islam became firmly established. Prayer was instituted, the alms tax and fasting were prescribed, legal punishments fixed, the forbidden and the permitted prescribed, and Islam took up its abode with them" (*Sira*, 346). The Sharia system was taking shape.

It was also during this time that tensions between Muhammad and the Jews and Christians started to crystalize into the patterns of animosity that would sculpt much of the history of the next millennium and a half. A novice student of Islam might be surprised and reassured to read all the Biblical references in the *Koran*. The

Torah, Jews, Christians, and many famous Biblical characters like Adam, Noah, Abraham, Lot, Moses, David, Solomon, Jonah, Mary, and Jesus are all mentioned favorably. Unfortunately, it is rare to find someone who has read both the *Bible* and the *Koran*. Those who have will quickly realize that the "*Bible*" stories told by Muhammad bear some marked discrepancies with the tales told in the *Bible* itself — and the Jews and Christians of Medina caught this.

The stories and personalities of the *Bible* were already well-known by a large segment of the population in the Middle East. This made it a useful tool to Muhammad for establishing his place in the divine plan. The problem was that the details kept getting in the way. Muhammad wanted all the stories, prophets, and prophecies to point to the coming of the greatest and final prophet: namely, him. But the stories just weren't written that way; so, he changed them. When the Jews and Christians of Medina called him on it, he said that Allah had revealed to him that, in fact, they were the ones who had changed the stories in order to conceal his coming for their own purposes. "It was the Jewish rabbis who used to annoy the apostle with questions and introduce confusion, so as to confound the truth with falsity" (*Sira*, 351). The claim was "that the people of the scriptures have changed with their own hands what was revealed to them and they have said (as regards their changed Scriptures): This is from Allah, in order to get some worldly benefit thereby" (Bukhari, 3:850). For example, Muhammad claimed that when God gave the Torah to Moses, He didn't just give it to him alone but also to a group of elders who accompanied Moses. These elders complained, "Something has come between us and the vision of God so let us hear His word when He speaks to thee. Moses conveyed the request to God who said: Yes, command them to purify themselves or to purify their clothing and to fast; and they did so. Then he brought them forth to the mountain, and when the cloud covered them Moses commanded them to prostrate themselves and his Lord spoke to him and they heard His voice giving them commands and prohibitions so that they understood what they heard. Then he went back with them to the Children of Israel and when he came to them a party of them changed the commandments they had been given; and when Moses said to the Children of Israel, 'God has ordered you to do so-and-so,' they contradicted him and said that God had ordered something else" (*Sira*, 369-370). In other words, according to Muhammad, what is recorded in the *Bible* is not what God directed, but what both Jewish and Christian leaders had contrived for their own purposes — including the concealment of the fact that a last and greatest prophet was coming to instruct and lead the faithful in living proper, worshipful lives.

Strong's Exhaustive Concordance of the Bible is a comprehensive concordance which records where any word in the *Bible* can be found in both the Old and New Testaments. If you were to look up "Muhammad" or "Mohammed" or any other version of the spelling of this name, you will find nothing. He's not mentioned, period. Now, that probably doesn't come as a surprise to Christians and Jews. What would come as a shocker is the claim that Muhammad is mentioned in Scripture; and not only that he is mentioned, but that he is presented as the climax of God's spiritual work here on earth. But this is precisely what Muslims believe and what they teach. Consider this passage: A faithful follower was asked, "'Tell me about the description of Allah's Apostle which is mentioned in Torah (i.e. Old Testament.)' He replied, 'Yes. By Allah, he is described in Torah with some of the qualities attributed to him in the Quran as follows: 'O Prophet! We have sent you as a witness (for Allah's True religion) And a giver of glad tidings (to the faithful believers), And a warner (to the unbelievers) And guardian of the illiterates. You are My slave and My messenger (i.e. Apostle). I have named you 'Al-Mutawakkil' (who depends upon Allah). You are neither discourteous, harsh Nor a noise-maker in the markets And you do not do evil to those Who do evil to you, but you deal With them with forgiveness and kindness. Allah will not let him (the Prophet) Die till he makes straight the crooked people by making them say: 'None has the right to be worshipped but Allah,' With which will be opened blind eyes And deaf ears and enveloped hearts'" (Bukhari, 3:335). By the way, this character, "Al-Mutawakkil," a reference to Muhammad, is not mentioned in the *Bible* either.

Students of the Old Testament will recall a couple of occasions where Abraham passed off Sarah as his sister, not his wife. Muhammad relates the story as well, but with a bit of a twist that may not be so familiar to the Old Testament scholars. According to Muhammad, Sarah, fearful that one of the kings who thought she was "available" would force himself on her, "performed ablution, prayed and said, 'O Allah! If I have believed in You and Your Apostle [Muhammad], and have saved my private parts from everybody except my husband, then please do not let this pagan overpower me' (Bukhari, 3:420). So, Sarah, who lived about 2,500 years before the time of Muhammad and the establishment of Islam, already referred to God as "Allah" and knew about his "Apostle" Muhammad. You can see why the Christians and Jews of his time had a little trouble with this.

Muhammad maintained that all true Jews and Christians were Muslims. These are the so-called "People of the Book" who know the real story of the *Bible*, but there aren't many of them. Of course, this means that the vast majority of those who call themselves Jews and Christians are really unrepentant infidels — Kafirs. To be sure, it will not go well with them. "God's curse is on the unbelievers…They have incurred anger upon anger and for the unbelievers there is a shameful punishment" (*Sira*, 374).

*   *   *

Another critical development was initiated during the period of the Medinan exile. It would create the model for Islamic expansion in the future and change the course of history: Jihad.

The first year in Medina was a difficult time of impoverishment and struggle for Muhammad and his Muslims. But then, a new revelation came to him, and he tried a different tactic based upon it. He began to send out raiding parties to rob the caravans of his old tribe, the Quraysh. Suddenly flush with money, which he generously shared with those who fought with him, Muhammad also found a way to entice new adherents: plunder.

"The apostle had not been given permission to fight or allowed to shed blood" up to this point (*Sira*, 313). But then Allah "gave permission to His apostle to fight and to protect himself against those who wronged them and treated them badly." (*Sira*, 313) This changed everything. The fact is that during his thirteen years at Mecca, Muhammad was a nearly complete failure as a religious leader. Only a few score converts were won to Muhammad's new religion based merely upon his and its appeal. Some scholars estimate that the total number of Muslim converts during these years may not have exceeded three hundred. Others calculated a much lower number. "The total number of those who migrated to Abyssinia, apart from the little children whom they took with them or were born to them there, was eighty-three men if Ammar b. Yasir was among them, but that is doubtful" (*Sira*, 215). The number who migrated to Medina was only about 150. Spiritual and intellectual persuasion have never proved to be Islam's strong points. Islam literally advanced by the edge of the sword; and now, Muhammad had Allah's permission to bloody the blade. Muslims were instructed to "Fight them (kafirs)… until God alone is worshipped" (*Sira*, 314). And so, "the apostle prepared for war in pursuance of God's command to fight his enemies…" (*Sira*, 415). "By Allah, whenever they heard about a caravan of Quraish heading towards Sham, they stopped it and attacked and killed them (i.e. infidels) and took their properties" (Bukhari, 3:891).

The following are excerpts from an account of one of these early raids. "A caravan of Quraysh carrying dry raisins and leather and other merchandise of Quraysh passed by them… Abdullah and his companions took the caravan and the two prisoners and came to Medina with them. One of Abdullah's family mentioned that he said to his companions, 'A fifth of what we have taken belongs to the apostle.' (This was before God had appointed a fifth of the booty to him.) So he set apart for the apostle a fifth of the caravan, and divided the rest among his companions" (*Sira*, 425). You see, not only had Allah told Muhammad that it was okay to fight on His behalf, "Allah's Apostle [also] said, 'Booty has been made legal for me'" (*Sira*, 484). So, god not only endorsed theft, he endorsed it by means of brutal force — plunder.

In Medina, Muhammad evolved from a failed religious leader into a successful warlord who employed economic warfare to weaken his enemies, fill his coffers, strike fear in the hearts of future targets (classic terrorism), entice new converts, and expand both his geographic and religious kingdom. It was here that he honed the model that would be used by subsequent generations of caliphs and Islamic leaders: use military force to seize the wealth of non-believers, kill or enslave the opposition, and use terror to "encourage" Kafirs to convert to Islam.

It was early in this evolution of Islam into a warrior cult that an important theological principle was established that would be critical throughout Islam's expansion. A band of Muslims raided a Quraysh caravan near a settlement named Nakhla. As usual, the raiders brought the plunder to Muhammad so he could take his cut, but the apostle initially refused saying, "I did not order you to fight in the sacred month" (*Sira*, 425). The attack had happened during the month of Rajab — one of four sacred months in the Islamic calendar. Fighting during these months was prohibited. Conveniently, Allah gave Muhammad a new revelation which would allow such attacks, even during the holy months. "They will question thee concerning the holy month, and fighting in it. Say: 'Fighting in it is a heinous thing, but to bar from God's way, and disbelief in Him, and the Holy Mosque, and to expel its people from it — that is more heinous in God's sight; and persecution is more heinous than slaying'" (*Koran*, 2:217). The theological principle that was introduced here is that any action which benefits Islam and Muslims is permissible, even if it violates other moral or secular laws.

*   *   *

One of the key contests between Muhammad's Muslims and the Quraysh took place at the Battle of Badr. Muhammad prevailed. Of the 314 who fought for Muhammad, 8 died (*Sira*, 506-507). Fifty of the Quraysh died, while 43 were taken prisoner (*Sira*, 511 & 515). Actually, accounts of the Quraysh casualties vary. Bukhari's Hadith, 4:276 states that "On the day (of the battle) of Badr, the Prophet and his companions had caused the Pagans to lose 140 men, seventy of whom were captured and seventy were killed." However, Ishaq's *Sira* actually offers itemized lists with names, and, therefore, may be considered more reliable.

Muhammad never forgot the lessons he learned while a businessman; he just applied them to his new business: religio-politics. Muhammad understood that there wasn't much economic value in a corpse, but a prisoner could be (1) seduced into becoming a Muslim through the offer of exchanging incarceration for "submission" (that is, accepting Islam), (2) ransomed to those who would pay for his freedom; or (3) sold into slavery. The last two of these created lucrative profit centers for Islam for centuries to come. Allah, according to Muhammad, even gave Muhammad special dispensation to engage in these egregious abuses of humanity. "God said, 'It is not for any prophet,' i.e. before thee, 'to take prisoners from his enemies'" but, "He made it lawful to him and to them as a mercy from Him and a gift from the Compassionate, the Merciful. He said, 'So enjoy what you have captured as lawful and good, and fear God" (*Sira*, 484). So, exactly how did this "compassionate" and "merciful" god intend for Muhammad and his Muslims to "enjoy" the people and property that had been captured? "I was given all-embracing words: booty was made lawful to me as to no prophet before me..." (*Sira*, 484). When the Battle of Badr was over, Muhammad "halted on the sandhill between the pass and al-Naziya called Sayar at a tree there and divided the booty which God had granted to the Muslims equally... the apostle divided the prisoners amongst his companions..." (*Sira*, 458-459). One of the prisoners was a man named Abu Aziz b. Umayr b. Hashim. Muhammad gave special instructions regarding him. "Bind him fast, for his mother is a wealthy woman; perhaps she will redeem him from you" (*Sira*, 459). The economics of kidnapping under Muhammad eventually became somewhat standardized. "The ransom of the polytheists was fixed at 4,000 dirhams per man, though some got off with 1,000" (Hisham, 3).

At the Battle of Badr, Muhammad's Muslims prevailed against superior numbers. It instilled a sense inevitability regarding the Muslims' quest, and it established a model of thinking and action that would guide Muslims when confronting non-believers right up to the present day. First, Allah will insure ultimate victory, even against overwhelming odds, to those who remain faithful. Second, the vanquished and their property are completely at the disposal of the victor — with no concern for conventional morality. Non-believers may be tortured, imprisoned, held for ransom, sold into slavery, or killed. Their property is booty to be distributed among the conquerors.

Muhammad's Muslims won a surprising victory at the Battle of Badr, but they suffered a significant defeat later at the Battle of Uhud, and Muhammad was wounded. It was the last defeat Muhammad would suffer.

Some time later, "A number of Jews who had formed a party against the apostle… went to Quraysh at Mecca and invited them to join them in an attack on the apostle so that they might get rid of him altogether… These words rejoiced Quraysh and they responded gladly to their invitation to fight the apostle, and they assembled and made their preparations" (*Sira*, 669). "When the apostle heard of heir intention he drew a trench about Medina…" (*Sira*, 670). This would come to be known as the Battle of the Trench or Ditch, named after the earthworks ordered by Muhammad to defend against the upcoming attack. The Muslims prevailed, but perhaps more importantly, the aggression against Muhammad's home base worked to cement an intractable hatred for the Jews, of whom he said, "These are they whom God hath cursed…" (*Sira*, 669). This hatred would later be manifested in the grizzly slaughter soon to be carried out at Medina.

Note: Muhammad claimed to accept the *Torah* — the first five books of the Old Testament — as the Book of God. In verse nine of Chapter Twenty-four of the fourth book of the *Torah*, "Numbers," God, speaking to the nation of Israel, says, "Blessed is he that blesseth thee, and cursed is he that curseth thee." Now, Muhammad claims that "These are they whom God hath cursed…." Logically, this means either that Muhammad is wrong, or God has

41

cursed Himself. Actually, as we have seen, Muhammad had skillfully crafted a convenient escape hatch for a dilemma such as this. The Jews and Christians had re-written the true Bible to suit their own needs. Numbers 24:9 must be one of those instances.

More battles ensued. Not long after the Battle of the Trench or the Ditch (the Battle of Al-Khandaq), the angel "Gabriel came to the apostle wearing an embroidered turban and riding on a mule with a saddle covered with a piece of brocade... 'God commands you, Muhammad, to go to Bani Qurayza. ["Bani" means "sons of" or "tribe of."] I am about to go to them to shake their stronghold'" (*Sira*, 684). "The apostle besieged them for twenty-five nights until they were sore pressed and God cast terror into their hearts" (*Sira*, 685). Confronted with inevitable defeat and aware of the Muslim's reputation for brutal-ity toward their vanquished, the Jews of Bani Qurayza sought terms of surrender, hoping to spare as many lives as possible. The apostle "of God, the Merciful, the Compassionate" ordered "that the men should be killed, the property divided, and the women and children tak-en as captives" (*Sira*, 689). "Then they surrendered, and the apostle confined them in Medina... Then the apostle went out to the market of Medina (which is still its market today) and dug trenches in it. Then he sent for them [the captured, male Jews] and struck off their heads in those trenches as they were brought out to him in batches... There were 600 or 700 in all, though some put the figure as high as 800 or 900" (*Sira*, 689-690). Muhammad had a twelve-year-old girl, Aisha, sit beside him to view the massacre. Any parent who committed such an act would be guilty of child abuse. Ah, but Muhammad wasn't this twelve-year-old's father. He was her husband. "Then the apostle divided the property, wives, and children of B. Qurayza among the Muslims, and he made known on that day the shares of horse and men, and took out the fifth…The apostle had chosen one of their women for himself…" (*Sira*, 692 & 693).

The violent raids of Islam continued, as did the killings, kidnappings, ransoming, enslaving, and taking "their wives, children, and property as booty" (*Sira*, 725). Before long, both sides — either because they were tired of the carnage or because they were attempting to buy time to plot their next attack — agreed to an armistice. The Muslims and members of the Quraysh tribe "agreed to lay aside war for ten years…[vowing that they] "will not show enmity one to another and there shall be no secret reservation or bad faith" (*Sira*, 747).

However, this did not stop Muhammad and the Muslims from raiding other communities and caravans. One of the most notorious (although Muslims would say "glorious") was the raid on Khaybar (another largely Jewish settlement) and its surroundings. Muhammad had received reports of a great stash of treasure in the area. Once again, his goal was plundering, not proselytizing. The Muslims prevailed again, and after the battle, "Kinana b. al-Rabi, who had the custody of the treasure of B. al-Nadir, was brought to the apostle who asked him about it. He denied that he knew where it was… the apostle gave orders to al-Zubayr b. al-Awwam, 'Torture him until you extract what he has,' so he kindled a fire with flint and steel on his chest until he was nearly dead. Then the apostle delivered him to Muhammad b. Maslama and he struck off his head, in revenge for his brother Mahmud [who had been killed in battle]" (*Sira*, 764).

One of the interesting developments from the Muslim conquest of Khaybar was the beginning of a practice known as "dhimmitude." "When the people of Khaybar surrendered … they asked the apostle to employ them on the property with half share in the produce, saying, 'We know more about it than you and we are better farmers.' The apostle agreed to this arrangement on the condition that 'if we wish to expel you we will expel you'" (*Sira*, 764). Always the shrewd businessman, Muhammad saw great potential in this suggestion. This would prove to be another way to extract wealth from captured people and to wear them down until they submitted to Islam.

"Dhimma" means compact or contract. A "dhimmi" is a "protected" person — specifically, a person protected by the terms of a contract. As compassionate and enlightened as this may sound, "dhimmi" is really is a euphemism for "indentured servant." A dhimmi is a Kafir who is allowed to dwell within a Muslim community, but under very strict control. For example, they have no civil rights, cannot testify in courts against Muslims, cannot practice their religion in public nor wear any religious symbols in public, and are taxed up to half of their wealth and income. Of course, all this suffering could end if the dhimmi merely submitted to Islam, which many eventually did.

As usual, the spoils from the victory at Khaybar were distributed according to a formula which always included one-fifth going to god's apostle. As has been the case with other warlord bands throughout history, the leader secured the loyalty of his followers by distributing a significant amount of the spoils to those who had participated in the battle. "The apostle gave gifts to those whose hearts were to be won over, notably the chiefs of the army, to win them and through them their people" (*Sira*, 880). This, also, was a great recruiting tool for inducing the poor and hopeless to join the ranks of the Muslims.

Of course, women were also part of the spoils, and Muhammad always had first choice. "When the apostle had conquered al-Quamus the fort of B. Abul-Huqayq [part of the Khaybar complex], Safiya d. Huyayy b. Akhtab was brought to him along with another woman…He gave orders that Safiya was to be put behind him and threw his mantle over her, so that the Muslims knew that he had chosen her for himself" (*Sira*, 763). The "apostle married Safiya in Khaybar… [even though he had] killed her father, her husband, and her people…" (*Sira*, 766).

*   *   *

The armistice that was supposed to secure peace between the Quraysh and the Muslims only lasted roughly two years. Acting on the pretext of a skirmish that had broken out between allies of the Quraysh and the Muslims, Muhammad mounted a major offensive against Mecca, the stronghold of the Quraysh tribe. "The Muslims who were present at the conquest of Mecca numbered 10,000…" (*Sira,* 828). Muhammad's forces prevailed, and "The apostle had instructed his commanders when they entered Mecca only to fight those who resisted them, except a small number who were to be killed even if they were found beneath the curtains of the Kaaba" (*Sira,* 818). Indeed, this very thing happened. "Allah's Apostle entered Mecca in the year of its Conquest wearing an Arabian helmet on his head and when the Prophet took it off, a person came and said, 'Ibn Khatal is holding the covering of the Ka'ba (taking refuge in the Ka'ba).' The Prophet said, 'Kill him'" (Bukhari, 3:72). Khatal had provoked Muhammad's ire back in the days when the Prophet still lived in Mecca, and he wasn't about to extend any grace — either to Khatal or others who worked for him. Ibn Khatal "had two singing-girls Fartana and her friend who used to sing satirical songs about the apostle, so he ordered that they should be killed with him" (*Sira,* 819).

Muhammad was a vengeful man who rarely let the gender of the culprit stop him from exacting a toll for opposing him. Later in his life he was offended by a verse written by a woman. "When the apostle heard what she had said he said, 'Who will rid me of Marwan's daughter?' Umayr b. Adiy al-Khatmi who was with him heard him, and that very night he went to her house and killed her.

In the morning he came to the apostle and told him what he had done and he said, 'You have helped God and His apostle, O Umayr!" Muhammad's record, however, indicated that he was quite content to be a hands-on executor of justice — or, in this case, a "hands-off" executor. When some men killed one of Muhammad's shepherds, "The apostle sent Kurz b. Jabir in pursuit and he overtook them and brought them to the apostle as he returned from the raid of Dhu Qarad. He cut off their hands and feet and gouged out their eyes" (Sira, 999). What remained of the still-living bodies was deposited in an especially harsh portion of desert where the victims ultimately died of thirst.

Some complained that it was not lawful to kill inside the holy city of Mecca. Once again, Muhammad claimed a special dispensation from Allah allowing him to do what others could not. "The apostle arose and addressed us, saying, 'God made Mecca holy the day He created heaven and earth, and it is the holy of holies until the resurrection day. It is not lawful for anyone who believes in God and the last day to shed blood therein, nor to cut down trees therein. It was not lawful to anyone before me and it will not be lawful to anyone after me. Indeed, it is not lawful for me except at this time because of (God's) anger against its people. Now it has regained its former holiness. Let those here now tell those that are not here. If anyone should say, 'The apostle killed men in Mecca', say God permitted His apostle to do so but He does not permit you" (Sira, 823-824).

CHAPTER FIVE

THE TRIUMPHAL RETURN TO MECCA

And so, about ten years after being chased out of Mecca, Muhammad returned as a conqueror. Not long after Mecca was secured, Muhammad's forces continued their religious war of aggression, conquest, submission, plunder, torture, and murder. "The apostle sent out troops in the district round Mecca inviting men to God; he did not order them to fight" (*Sira*, 833). Although these "missionaries" were not ordered to fight, blood still flowed. Khalid b. al-Walid was dispatched to the "lower part of the flat country" where he "subdued" some of the population. (*Sira*, 833) "As soon as they had laid down their arms Khalid ordered their hands to be tied behind their backs and put them to the sword, killing a number of them" (*Sira*, 834). Upon hearing this, Muhammad essentially washed his hands of any responsibility for the slaughter, but he allowed Khalid to continue his "missionary" work.

The raids continued, Muhammad's army grew, and his ambitions swelled. "The apostle stayed in Medina from Dhul-Hijja to Rajab [from the twelfth to the seventh month in the Islamic calendar], and then gave orders to prepare to raid the Byzantines" (*Sira*, 893). This was only roughly a year after the occupation of Mecca. He also sent an emissary "to convoke the Arabs to war on Syria" (*Sira*, 984). The ends of the earth were the only limits to the aggressive ambitions of Islam and its founder.

"Tabuk was the last raid that the apostle made" (*Sira*, 929). His life was drawing near an end. He would attend one more hajj. "[B]etween the time of his coming to Medina and his death," Muhammad oversaw the execution of thirty-eight raids and battles. He personally took part in twenty-seven of them (*Sira*, T.1575 & 973). When Muhammad did not personally command a raid, he entrusted leadership to one of his "Companions," as his closest aids were known. For example, Zayd b. Haritha led the raid on B. Fazara. One result of this battle was that Umm Qirfa was captured. "She was a very old woman, wife of Malik [who was killed in the battle]. Her daughter and Abdullah b. Masada were also taken. Zayd ordered Qays b. al-Musahhar to kill Umm Qirfa and he killed her cruelly... by putting a rope to her two legs and the two camels and driving them until they rent her in two" (*Sira*, 980).

At about the age of sixty-two, "the apostle began to suffer from the illness by which God took him to what honor and compassion He intended for him shortly before the end of Safar or in the beginning of Rabi ul-Awwal [the second and third months in the Islamic calendar]" (*Sira*, 999). Muhammad's young wife, Aisha, reported, "When the ailment of the Prophet became aggravated and his disease became severe, he asked his wives to permit him to be nursed (treated) in my house. So they gave him the permission. Then the Prophet came (to my house) with the support of two men, and his legs were dragging on the ground, between Abbas, and the other man" (Bukhari, 1:197). "Then the apostle's illness worsened and he suffered much pain" (*Sira*, 1006). On the day he died, his wife, "Aisha said: The apostle came back to me from the mosque that day and lay in my bosom... And so the apostle was taken... It was due to my ignorance and extreme youth that the apostle died in my arms. Then I laid his head on a pillow and got up beating my breast and slapping my face along with the other women" (*Sira*, 1011).

"[T]he last injunction the apostle gave was in his words 'Let not two religions be left in the Arabian peninsula.' The apostle died on the 12th of Rabi ul-Awwal on the very day that he came to Medina as an emigrant, having completed exactly twelve years in his migration" (*Sira*, 1021).

The prophet's mantle of authority passed to Abu Bakr, the man who had made his young daughter, Aisha, a present to Muhammad. "Thereupon the people swore fealty to Abu Bakr as a body after the pledge in the hall" (*Sira*, 1017). [The Shia contend that Ali was, in fact, Muhammad's first legitimate successor.] "When fealty had been sworn to Abu Bakr men came to prepare the apostle for burial on the Tuesday" (*Sira*, 1018). "The Muslims had disputed over the place of burial... Abu Bakr said, 'I heard the apostle say, "No prophet dies but he is buried where he died."'; so the bed on which he died was taken up and they made a grave beneath it... The apostle was buried in the middle of the night of the Wednesday" (*Sira*, 1019-1020).

Muhammad was one of those dynamic personalities who changed the course of history. It always remains to be seen, however, which way the flow will continue after the passing of such a personality. The future of Islam was quickly challenged after the apostle's death. "Abu Ubayda and other traditionalists told me [Ibn Hisham] that when the apostle was dead most of the Meccans meditated withdrawing from Islam and made up their minds to do so. Attab b. Asid went in such fear of them that he hid himself. Then Suhayl b. Amr arose and after giving thanks to God mentioned the death of the apostle and said, 'That will increase Islam in force. If anyone troubles us we will cut off his head.' Thereupon the people abandoned their intention and Attab reappeared once more" (Hisham, 920). Islam was founded on the edge of the sword and it would be preserved by the edge of the sword. The main motivation to become and stay a Muslim throughout history has not been the conviction of the believer; it has been his survival instinct. Join or die. Stay or die. It can easily be argued that a substantial number — perhaps most — of Muslims are hostages within their own religion.

*   *   *

Before concluding this brief summary of the life of Muhammad, there is another area of his life that is revealing: his wives. At the time of Muhammad, four wives was considered to be an allowable maximum. "If you fear that you will not act justly towards the orphans, marry such women as seem good to you, two, three, four; but if you fear you will not be equitable, then only one, or what your right hands own; so it is likelier you will not be partial" (*Koran*, 4:3). But, as we have seen in other areas, Allah often smiled upon his apostle allowing him to live by a different set of rules from others. "He married thirteen women..." (Hisham, 918). Conveniently, Allah provided another exemption for his messenger in nothing less than a divine download given to Muhammad for inclusion in the *Koran*: "O Prophet, We have made lawful for thee thy wives whom thou hast given their wages and what thy right hand owns, spoils of war that God has given thee..." (*Koran*, 33:50). Two of Muhammad's wives were taken from among captured populations. "He married Juwayriya d. al-Harith b. Abu Dirar al-Khuzaiya who was among the captives of B. Mustaliq of Khuzaa... "He married Safiya d. Huyay b. Akhtab whom he had captured at Khaybar and chosen for himself" (Hisham, 918).

His favorite wife, however, was reputed to have been Aisha, who was a gift from his devoted "Companion" Abu Bakr, Aisha's father. Muhammad "married Aisha when she was a girl of six years of age, and he consummated that marriage when she was nine years old" (Bukhari, 5:63;3896). Muhammad was in his early fifties. Another traditionist gives slightly different details, but the story is still basically the same: "He married Aisha in Mecca when she was a child of seven and lived with her in Medina when she was nine or ten. She was the only virgin that he married. Her father, Abu Bakr, married her to him and the apostle gave her four hundred dirhams" (Hisham, 918). [It is interesting to note that her wedding gift was one tenth the standard ransom for a "polytheist," or Christian.]

Muhammad has occasionally been depicted as a pedophile. His relationship with Aisha is the primary basis for this accusation. Let's look at the facts. Muhammad received this wife as a gift and married her when she was six or seven years old. He "consummated" the marriage when she was nine. At the age of twelve, the apostle had her sit beside him and witness the beheading of between six hundred and nine hundred Jews after the battle of Qurayza. To put this in contemporary terms, Muhammad married a first-grader, deflowered her as a third-grader, and compelled her to view a savage atrocity as a sixth-grader. I'll let the reader decide what word best describes such a person. Some apologists may try to excuse this behavior by saying that such marriage practices were not unheard-of back in Seventh Century Arabia. This argument doesn't get our Founding Fathers off the hook for occasionally participating in slavery, which was still common practice in the Eighteenth Century. Respect for humankind knows no time period.

The accounts of the Hadiths sometimes seemingly contradict the information above regarding the number of Muhammad's wives. For example, "Anas bin Malik said, 'The Prophet used to visit all his wives in a round, during the day and night and they were eleven in number... and Said said on the authority of Qatada that Anas had told him about nine wives only (not eleven)" (Bukhari, 1:268). This confusion is probably clarified by Ibn Hisham who wrote, "The apostle consummated his marriage with eleven women, two of whom died before him, namely Khadija and Zaynab. He died, leaving the nine we have mentioned. With two, he had no marital relations, namely Asthma d. al-human, the Kindite woman, whom he married and found to be suffering from leprosy and so returned to her people with a suitable gift; and Amra d. Yazid, the Kilab woman who was recently an unbeliever. When she came to the apostle, she said, 'I seek God's protection against you,' and he replied that one who did that was inviolable so he sent her back to her people" (Hisham, 918). It seems most likely, therefore, that Muhammad married thirteen women, two preceded him in death, and two were discharged. Accordingly, at any given time during the later portion of his life, Muhammad probably had between nine and eleven wives living with him. None, however, provided him with a living male child to succeed him — a matter of shame in the Arabic culture. However, a Coptic [Egyptian Christian] sex slave named Mary or Marium did give him a son named Ibrahim.

*   *   *

Murderous violence, stealing, kidnapping for ransom, rape, vengeance, terror, and the slave trade have been a significant part of Islam's standard operating procedures from the very beginning — facts which their own autho-rized texts confirm — and Muhammad set the example. "[F]ight everyone in the way of God and kill those who disbelieve in God" (*Sira*, 992).

Over the course of roughly the last nine years of Muhammad's life, he personally attended twenty-seven raids. His Muslims conducted another thirty-eight battles and expeditions. This means that Muhammad directed vi-olent actions at a rate of about one every seven weeks — not counting executions and assassinations. It also has been estimated that the religion and politics of Islam have resulted in the deaths of approximately 270 million people; consisting of about 60 million Christians, 80 million Hindus, 10 million Buddhists, and 120 million Africans of various religions. (Bill Warner, *Mohammad and the Unbelievers*, CSPI Publishing, 2010, p. 160)

An essential conclusion from this review of Muhammad's life is that violence and "terror" are not the tactics of "radical" Muslims; they are the tactics of Muslims, and they are endorsed by Allah. "...then God came upon them from whence they had not reckoned, and He cast terror into their hearts…" (*Koran*, 59:2). "Then God said, 'Then thy Lord revealed to the angels, I am with you so strengthen those that believe.' i.e. help those that believe. 'I will cast terror into the hearts of those who disbelieve, so strike off their heads and cut off all their fingers, because they opposed God and His apostle and he who opposes God and His apostle, (will find) God severe in punishment" (*Sira*, 477). This quotation from *Sirat Rasul Allah* essentially reiterates verses from the eighth "Sura" of the *Koran*: "When thy Lord was revealing to the angels, 'I am with you; so confirm the believers. I shall cast into the unbelievers' hearts terror; so smite above the necks, and smite every finger of them!' That, because they had made a breach with God and with his Messenger; and whosoever makes a breach with God and with His Messenger, surely God is terrible in retribution" (*Koran* 8:12-14). Allah repeats his command to deal severely with unbelievers a little later in the *Sira*. "'If you come upon them in war, deal with them so forcibly as to terrify those who follow them, haply they may take warning,' i.e. make a severe example of them to those that come after, that haply they may understand. 'And prepare what strength you can against them, and cavalry by which you may strike terror into the enemy of God and your enemy' as far as His words, 'And whatever you spend in the way of God will be repaid to you: you will not be wronged,' i.e. you will not lose your reward with God in the next life and a rapid recompense in this world.' Then He said, 'And if they incline to peace incline thou to it,' i.e. if they ask you for peace on the basis of Islam then make peace on that basis…" (*Sira*, 482). In short, be terrifying in war, and only agree to peace if it suits the interests of Islam.

Muhammad was not merely a vicious warlord; he also was a clever businessman who incorporated the economic principles of piracy to fund and grow his empire. As a warlord, he deployed his armies to spread Islam by the edge of the sword. If you resisted, he would strike with the savage tools of military aggression to kill, torture, rob, rape, ransom, and enslave. But Muhammad was not just brutal, he was shrewd. He employed a clever mix of terror and clemency to win adherents. "If you have any use for your life then come quickly to the apostle, for he does not kill anyone who comes to him in repentance" (*Sira*, 887). The rewards of repentance, however, were not reserved merely for the afterlife. If you joined the Muslim marauders, you also would join in the Muslim plunder.

Of course, there is far more to the life of Muhammad than has been covered in this brief overview. Although his brutal nature has been well-documented, he also exhibited compassionate and benevolent traits. For example, there are hadiths which tell of a transaction between Muhammad and another man who was having trouble with his camel. Muhammad "cured" the problem and then offered to buy the camel. Upon hearing that the man was preparing to marry, Muhammad paid the man for the camel, then graciously let him keep the animal (Bukhari, 4:211). And, although accounts vary, it seems that despite all the booty he collected over the course of his many battles, Muhammad died leaving a modest inheritance. "The Prophet did not leave behind him after his death, anything except his arms, his white mule, and a piece of land at Khaibar [Khaybar] which he left to be given in charity" (Bukhari, 4:160).

There are also accounts of miracles being performed by Muhammad. Once, when Muhammad asked for his companion, Ali, to be brought to him, "Someone informed him that he was suffering from eye-trouble. So, he ordered them to bring Ali in front of him. Then the Prophet spat in his eyes and his eyes were cured immediately as if he had never any eye-trouble." [Christian readers familiar with the Gospel accounts of Jesus may be experiencing a touch of deja-vu right about now.] On the other hand, we also could point to some hadiths which tell of Muhammad being "bewitched" and exhibiting strange behavior. "Once the Prophet was bewitched so that he began to imagine that he had done a thing which in fact he had not done" (Bukhari, 4:400). Another hadith gives this account: "Magic was worked on the Prophet so that he began to fancy that he was doing a thing which he was not actually doing. One day he invoked (Allah) for a long period and then said, 'I feel that Allah has inspired me as how to cure myself. Two persons came to me (in my dream) and sat, one by my head and the other by my feet. One of them asked the other, "What is the ailment of this man?" The other replied, "He has been bewitched." The first asked,

"Who has bewitched him?" The other replied, "Lubaid bin Al-Asam." The first one asked, "What material has he used?" The other replied, "A comb, the hair gathered on it, and the outer skin of the pollen of the male date-palm." The first asked, "Where is that?" The other replied, "It is in the well of Dharwan.'" So, the Prophet went out towards the well and then returned and said to me on his return, "Its date-palms (the date-palms near the well) are like the heads of the devils." I asked, 'Did you take out those things with which the magic was worked?' He said. 'No, for I have been cured by Allah and I am afraid that this action may spread evil amongst the people.' Later on the well was filled up with earth" (Bukhari, 4:490). Modern-day psychologists would probably use terms other than "bewitched" to describe the Prophet's behavior; but they all would boil down to some form of serious pathology.

The purpose of this book, however, is not to provide a comprehensive documentary on the life of Muhammad. Rather, it aims to alert the non-Muslim world to the things it needs to know in order to understand and successfully relate to the Muslim world. In a nutshell, here it is: Islam is all about Muhammad. He is the exemplar. He is the model for Muslim beliefs and behavior. If Muhammad said it, you must believe it. If Muhammad did it, you can — even must — do it, too.

Everything a Muslim knows about Allah came from Muhammad. The alleged divine downloads in the *Koran* came through Muhammad. The narratives in *Sirat Rasul*

Allah and the *Hadith* all document Muhammad's words and actions so they can be emulated. Furthermore, according to Muhammad, the only "accurate" version of Biblical scripture comes from Muhammad. Yes, it's all about Muhammad, and basically, he was a vicious warlord who used a religion of his own conjuring to justify his tyranny and extend it to successive generations.

Yes, if you want to understand Islam, do not study the *Koran*. Study the life of Muhammad. Islam is Muhammad, and Muhammad is Islam. Far beyond the theology of Islam, the life of Muhammad will give you a clear perception of what is to come if Islam is allowed to spread. By studying the life of Muhammad, you will pull back the curtain on the coming terror. If you are a Kafir, your options are simple and stark: submit and convert, or be subject to slavery, robbery, rape, torture, and murder. Those were the options Muhammad gave to the infidel, and nothing has changed. So, infidel, unless you plan to convert, be enslaved, or die, the only course left for you is to fight. "Coexist" is not an option.

PART THREE

ISLAM

CHAPTER SIX

SURRENDER AND DO GOOD

"The true religion with God is Islam" (Koran, 3:19).

"Allah's Apostle said, 'We (Muslims) are the last (people to come in the world) but (will be) the foremost (on the Day of Resurrection)'" (Bukhari, 1:239).

"Islam" is an Arabic word meaning "submission" or "surrender." It is a very appropriate name for this religion, for it insists upon complete submission from its adherents to the point of slavery. Slavery, in fact, is the final destination for all mortals, one way or another. A faithful Muslim is a "slave of Allah." Muhammad once recounted a tale about angels returning to Allah after observing humans to see how well they performed their prayers. Allah's greeting to the angels was "In what state did you leave my slaves?" (Bukhari, 1:530). And for those who do not accept Islam, slavery and death await them in this life, as well as eternal damnation and punishment in the next life.

Slavery was part and parcel of Muhammad's existence. His father was named "Abdullah," which means "servant" or "slave of Allah." Muhammad often referred to himself as a slave of Allah. As we have seen, Muhammad eagerly adopted the institution of slavery in order to more completely terrorize and exploit his opponents. And as we will see later, Islam has played a starring role in the tragic tale of global slavery for nearly fourteen hundred years.

The idea of submission in some form or another is not uncommon in religions, including Christianity. For example, the apostle Paul repeatedly referred to himself as a "doulos" of Christ. The Greek word "doulos" refers to a slave, bondsman, or servant. However, there is an important distinction between what Muhammad and Paul meant about bondage. The Greek word "doulos" refers to a person who has chosen the status of a servant, not one who has it imposed upon him. Paul **chose** to define himself as a "doulos" of Jesus Christ. Allah and Muhammad imposed the status on all humankind. The name of a popular Christian hymn is *I Surrender All*. Christian submission, however, leads to emancipation from the bondage of sin and a liberating sense of joy. Islamic submission, on the other hand, results in the bondage of endlessly repeating the same earthly rituals which allegedly leads to paradise.

Let us now briefly summarize the main elements of Islamic theology, and then we will go on to consider the Five Pillars of Islam.

God the Creator.

"God is the Creator of every thing; He is Guardian over every thing; unto Him belong the keys of the heavens and the earth. And those who disbelieve in the signs of God, those — they are the losers" (*Koran* 39:62-3).

God is One.

"Your God is One God; there is no god but He…" (*Koran* 2:163). Muslims, Jews, and Christians are all mono-theists; that is, they believe in one God. The Christian belief, however, is a bit more complicated. They believe in one God in three Persons: Father, Son, and Holy Spirit, or Holy Ghost. Christians call this the "Trinity," but Muslims call it "poly-theism." To Muslims, Trinitarianism is a belief in multiple gods. Muhammad believed that Jesus was a great prophet, but not divine; he claimed that he was instructed by Allah "to warn those who say God has taken a son" (*Sira*, 193).

God is Righteous.

Allah is righteous and deserves a righteous response. "True piety is this: to believe in God, and the Last Day, the angels, the Book, and the Prophets, to give of one's substance, however cherished, to kinsmen, and orphans, the needy, the traveller, beggars, and to ransom the slave, to perform the prayer, to pay the alms. And they who fulfill their covenant when they have engaged in a covenant, and endure with fortitude misfortune, hardship and peril, these are they who are true in their faith, these are the truly godfearing" (*Koran*, 2:177).

God the Judge.

Like most other religions except Christianity, Islam teaches that the performance of good deeds (works) is necessary in order to earn righteousness and the entitlement to enter Paradise. Allah ultimately will judge how well each person did and whether he or she warrants Paradise or Hell. The Islamic faith holds that Allah sent Muhammad "as an apostle. 'To give those who believe, **who do good works**, the good news that they will have a glorious reward, enjoying it everlastingly,' i.e. the eternal abode" (*Sira*, 193; emphasis added). Muhammad said, "Verily! **good deeds remove (annul) the evil deeds**" (Bukhari 1:504; emphasis added). Virtually the same words are used in the *Koran* where it states, "surely the good deeds will drive away the evil deeds" (*Koran*, 11:114). A traditionist tells this story: "One day while the Prophet was sitting in the company of some people, (the angel) Gabriel came and asked... 'What is Islam?' Allah's Apostle replied, 'To worship Allah Alone and none else, to offer prayers **perfectly** to pay the compulsory charity (Zakat) and to observe fasts during the month of Ramadan'" (Bukhari, 1:47; emphasis added). Muhammad further said, "The reward of deeds depends upon the intention and every person will get the reward according to what he has intended" (Bukhari, 1:51). So, not only must one perform the required deeds properly (more on this shortly), he must have good intentions while doing them.

All this suggests that, in effect, Allah keeps a scale in which he weighs a person's good deeds on one side against his bad deeds on the other. One must amass sufficient good deeds to nullify the bad ones. An excellent example of how this works is illustrated in the following hadith. "Allah's Apostle said, 'If one says one-hundred times in one day: "None has the right to be worshipped but Allah, the Alone Who has no partners, to him belongs Dominion and to Him belong all the Praises, and He has power over all things (i.e. Omnipotent)", one will get the reward of manumitting [freeing] ten slaves, and one-hundred good deeds will be written in his account, and one-hundred bad deeds will be wiped off or erased from his account, and on that day he will be protected from the morning till evening from Satan, and nobody will be superior to him except one who has done more than that which he has done'" (Bukhari, 4:514).

Now, compare Islam's accounting system with the Christian concept of grace proclaimed in Ephesians 2:8-9. "For it is by grace you have been saved, through faith — and this not from yourselves, it is the gift of God — not by works [deeds], so that no one can boast" (NIV). In Christianity, salvation is not achieved simply by performing a sufficient number of good deeds in order to counter balance the total number of bad deeds committed during a lifetime. Salvation comes from having faith in an act of divine love and grace; namely, accepting Jesus as Savior. God is pure and righteous, and His home is pure and righteous. No number of good deeds can possibly cleanse us from the spiritual filth of the sins we have committed, and this filth locks us out of Heaven. But God's love for us — His **children** — is so great that He sacrificed His only Son in order to unlock the gate of Heaven and bring us home. Jesus paid a debt which He did not owe because we owed a debt we could never repay. It is in this way, and only in this way, that God's forgiveness and personal salvation can be achieved. To be sure, God appreciates our good deeds, but they could never be sufficient to deserve Heaven. Only the Father's love is great enough to do that. It is a beautiful story of Paternal tenderness and devotion which a Muslim — Allah's **slave** — could never appreciate.

According to the tenets of Islam, after one's time here on Earth has concluded, "Every soul shall be paid in full for what it has wrought; and He knows very well what they do. Then the unbelievers shall be driven in companies into Gehenna [Hell] till, when they have come thither, then its gates will be opened and its keepers will say to them, 'Did not Messengers come to you from among yourselves, reciting to you the signs of your Lord and warning you against the encounter of this your day?' They shall say, 'Yes indeed; but the word of the chastisement has been realized against the unbelievers.' It shall be said, 'Enter the gates of Gehenna, to dwell therein forever.'

How evil is the lodging of those that are proud! Then those that feared their Lord shall be driven in companies into Paradise, till, when they have come thither, and its gates are opened, and its keepers will say to them, 'Peace be upon you! Well you have fared; enter in, to dwell forever.' And they shall say, 'Praise belongs to God, who has been true in His promise to us, and has bequeathed upon us the earth, for us to make our dwelling wheresoever we will in Paradise'" (*Koran* 39:70-4).

God is Knowable — Sort of.

According to Muhammad, Allah has revealed enough about his desires to make it possible for us humans (slaves) to know how we are supposed to act. This special revelation, as some Christian theologians would put it, comes from studying the *Koran* as well as the life of Muhammad, the perfect Muslim model. But do not deduce from this that there is one, universal, and eternal standard of right and wrong, like in the Judeo-Christian tradition. Like the Roman god Janus, who faces in opposite directions at the same time, Islamic morality also looks two ways at the same time. There is a distinct duality in Islam that holds that acts are neither good nor bad just because "they are." The righteousness or malevolence of deeds is rooted heavily in why they are committed; and generally speaking, if something is done to further the interests of Islam, that's okay with Allah. Lying, cheating, stealing, torturing, raping, kidnapping, enslaving, killing, etc., are wrong if

Muslims do these things to other Muslims, but perfectly permissible if done to Kafirs — just as the perfect Muslim model, Muhammad, did.

More on duality later. For now, the point is that Allah's desires for and from humans (slaves) is knowable as long as you view him through the lenses of Islam — all of which were ground and polished by Muhammad. The *Koran* provides divine revelations — as presented by Muhammad. The *Sira* and *Hadith* provide guidelines — as performed by Muhammad. Even the *Bible* reveals the will of Allah, as long as you read it correctly — that is, you guessed it, as interpreted by Muhammad. You see, Muslims, as instructed by Muhammad, believe that Allah gave Moses the "Book" (the *Torah*, or book of laws), inspired the writing of other portions of what we call the Old Testament (the books of history, poetry, and prophets), and authored the Gospel of the New Testament. "He has sent down upon thee the Book with the truth, confirming what was before it, and He sent down the Torah and the Gospel aforetime, as guidance to the people, and He sent down the Salvation" (*Koran*, 3:3). "We believe in God, and that which has been sent down on us, and sent down on Abraham and Ishmael, Isaac and Jacob, and the Tribes, and in that which was given to Moses and Jesus, and the Prophets, of their Lord; we make no division between any of them and to Him we surrender" (*Koran*, 3:84).

However, there is a catch, and it's a big one. Muhammad believed that throughout history, religious leaders — both Jews and Christians — corrupted true Scripture for their own purposes. They are "Those who conceal what the Book God has sent down on them, and sell it for little price — they shall eat naught but the Fire in their bellies; God shall not speak to them on the Day of Resurrection neither purify them; there awaits them a painful chastisement" (*Koran,* 2:174). Consequently, you're not getting the true story when you go to the bookstore and buy a copy of the Bible. If you want to know what god — that is, Allah — really said, you'll have to listen to Muhammad, because the truth was revealed to him.

Yes, the lenses of Islam — the spiritual eyeglasses to be used for viewing everything — were ground and polished by Muhammad. He is the sole purveyor of the Islamic worldview. Know him and you know Islam. Understand him and you can predict what Islamists will do.

Chastisement.

As might be expected from a religion that is "works"-oriented, Islam is big on punishment, or "chastisement." The words "chastise" and "chastisement" show up well over two hundred times in the *Koran.* (One search showed 231 entries, but the number will vary depending on the translation.) That works out to about once every three pages. Obviously, a significant theme — and motivator;

and the punishment is rarely so mild as a mere slap on the wrist. Consider the following:

> "As for those who disbelieve in God's signs, for them awaits a terrible chastisement; God is All-mighty, Vengeful" (*Koran* 3:4).
>
> "As for the unbelievers, for them garments of fire shall be cut, and there shall be poured over their heads boiling water whereby whatsoever is in their bellies and their skins shall be melted; for them await hooked iron rods; as often as they desire in their anguish to come forth from it, they shall be restored into it, and: 'Taste the chastisement of the burning!'" (*Koran*, 22:19-22).

As we have seen, Islam is very "works"-oriented. First and foremost, a person must accept Allah as god and Muhammad as his apostle. Without this precondition, even one's good deeds will be unavailing. According to Islam and Muhammad, there are five types of good deeds which must be performed in order to earn Paradise. These are called the "Five Pillars of Islam."

CHAPTER SEVEN

THE FIVE PILLARS OF ISLAM

"Allah's Apostle said: Islam is based on (the following) five (principles):

1. To testify that none has the right to be worshipped but Allah and Muhammad is Allah's Apostle.
2. To offer the (compulsory congregational) prayers dutifully and perfectly.
3. To pay Zakat (i.e. obligatory charity).
4. To perform Hajj (i.e. Pilgrimage to Mecca).
5. To observe fast during the month of Ramadan" (Bukhari, 1:7).

Let's explore each of these in more detail.

1. Shahada.

This word comes from the Arabic language and means "the testimony." It is the most basic creed of

Islam. In its shortest form it states, "There is no god but Allah, Muhammad is the messenger of God." Muslims are "Unitarian," not "Trinitarian" like Christians. Islam holds that a belief in one God in three Persons (Father, Son, and Holy Spirit) is "polytheism": a belief in many gods, which is blasphemous and idolatry. God — Allah — is one, and his last and greatest prophet is Muhammad. Muhammad is to be obeyed because he is god's faithful messenger. This is the first "Pillar of Islam."

2. Salat.

The practice of performing five, daily, ritual prayers is called "Salat." The faithful are to perform ablution, or ritual cleansing, before each prayer. They are to face in the direction of the Kaaba, which is located in the city of Mecca, Saudi Arabia. The direction one is to face while praying is called the "Qibla," and many Muslim homes and Mosques have a mark on the wall indicating this proper direction. Each prayer includes a given number of "rakat" (the singular form is "rakah"), which consists of prescribed actions and words. The *Sira* states that this model of ablution and prayer was given to Muhammad by the angel Gabriel (*Sira*, 158).

Performing the five daily prayers is mandatory among Muslims except for the prepubescent, those menstruating, or those who are experiencing bleeding during the forty days following childbirth. The timing of the prayers relates to the position of the sun. The "fajr" is performed near dawn. The "zuhr" takes place after midday. This is followed by the "asr" later in the afternoon; the "maghrib" after sunset; and the "isha" after nightfall. The exact timing and practice may vary depending upon the sect of Islam and the time of the year. Generally, the process takes about 15 to 20 minutes. If a salat is not performed at the prescribed time, it must be conducted later. The failure to pray can nullify one's good deeds. According to Muhammad, "Whoever misses the Asr prayer (intentionally) then it is as if he lost his family and property" (Bukhari, 1:527); and "Whoever leaves the Asr prayer, all his (good) deeds will be annulled" (Bukhari, 1:528 & 568).

The importance of performing these five daily prayers cannot be overstated. Muhammad said, "'If there was a river at the door of anyone of you and he took a bath in it five times a day would you notice any dirt on him?' They [the congregation] said, 'Not a trace of dirt would be left.' The Prophet added, 'That is the example of the five prayers with which Allah blots out (annuls) evil deeds'" (Bukhari, 1:506).

Muhammad believed that there is great power in prayer; namely, the power to blot out evil deeds and even to chase away the Devil. "Allah's Apostle said, 'When the Adhan is pronounced [the "Adhan" is the call to prayer pronounced before each of the five daily prayers] Satan takes to his heels and passes wind with noise during his flight in order not to hear the Adhan" (Bukhari, 1:582).

The powerful ritualism and "works" orientation of Islam is clearly evident in many of Muhammad's teachings about prayer, where slavish attention is paid to how prayers are to be performed. Prayer had to be done in the right way and at the right time. Variations could decrease or increase the benefit derived from the prayer. Although Muhammad once said, "The reward of deeds depends upon the intentions and every person will get the reward according to what he has intended" (Bukhari, 1:1), it is also true that "the reward of deeds depends upon the" perfection with which those deeds are performed. Consider the following remarks about prayer.

Muhammad said, "If the people knew the reward for the Zuhr prayer in its early time, they would race for it. If they knew the reward for the Isha and the Fajr prayers in congregation, they would join them even if they had to crawl. If they knew the reward for the first row, they would draw lots for it" (Bukhari, 1:688).

Arriving early for prayers on Friday was especially important. "The Prophet said, 'On every Friday the angels take their stand at every gate of the mosques to write the names of the people chronologically (i.e. according to the time of their arrival for the Friday prayer) and when the Imam sits (on the pulpit) they fold up their scrolls and get ready to listen to the sermon" (Bukhari, 4:433).

"Allah's Apostle said, 'If the Imam leads the prayer correctly then he and you will receive the rewards but if he makes a mistake (in the prayer) then you will receive the reward for the prayer and the sin will be his'" (Bukhari, 1:663).

"The Prophet said, 'The prayer offered in congregation is twenty-five times more superior (in reward) to the prayer offered alone in one's house or in a business center, because if one performs ablution [ritual washing] and does it perfectly, and then proceeds to the mosque with the sole intention of praying, then for each step which he takes towards the mosque, Allah upgrades him a degree in reward and (forgives) crosses out one sin till he enters the mosque. When he enters the mosque he is considered in prayer as long as he is waiting for the prayer and the angels keep on asking for Allah's forgiveness for him and they keep on saying "O Allah! Be merciful to him, O Allah! Forgive him, as long as he keeps on sitting at his praying place and does not pass wind"'" (Bukhari, 1:466).

And not only is congregational prayer better than prayer offered in one's house, "Allah's Apostle said, 'One prayer in my Mosque is better than one thousand prayers in any other mosque excepting Al-Masjid-Al-Haram [the "Sacred," "Grand," or "Great" Mosque in Mecca]'" (Bukhari, 2:282).

Muhammad's favorite wife, Aisha, passed on this tenet from Muhammad: "The things which annul the prayers were mentioned before me. They said, 'Prayer is annulled by a dog, a donkey and a woman (if they pass in front of the praying people)'" (Bukhari, 1:490). In fact, it is important to keep anyone from passing between you and your Qibla. "The Prophet said, 'If while you are praying, somebody intends to pass in front of you, prevent him; and should he insist, prevent him again; and if he insists again, fight with him (i.e. prevent him violently e.g.

pushing him violently), because such a person is (like) a devil'" (Bukhari, 4:495).

Even the physical position of the one offering the prayer could determine the effectiveness of the prayer. "The Prophet was ordered (by Allah) to prostrate on seven parts and not to tuck up the clothes or hair (while praying). Those parts are: the forehead (along with the tip of the nose), both hands, both knees, and (toes of) both feet" (Bukhari, 1:773). The same dictate applied to other Muslims as well, and the failure to position oneself properly could even nullify the effectiveness of the prayer. "I offered prayer beside my father and approximated both my hands and placed them in between the knees. My father told me not to do so and said, 'We used to do the same but we were forbidden (by the Prophet) to do it and were ordered to place the hands on the knees'" (Bukhari, 1:756). "Hudhaifa saw a person who was not performing the bowing and prostrations perfectly. He said to him. 'You have not prayed and if you should die you would die on a religion other than that of Muhammad'" (Bukhari, 1:757). Muhammad also said, "Know that the prayer of the sitter is only half as valuable as the prayer of the stander" (*Sira*, 415).

Interestingly enough, spitting during prayer was acceptable as long as one was careful about the direction in which he launched the spittle. Muhammad said, "Whenever any of you is in prayer he should know that Allah is in from of him. So none should spit in front of him in the prayer" (Bukhari, 1:720). Projectile saliva was to be directed to the left side. "The Prophet said, 'Whenever anyone of you is in prayer... he should neither spit in front of him nor on his right side but to his left side under his left foot'" (Bukhari, 2:305).

In Islam, even luck can play a big part in the forgiveness of one's sins. "The Prophet said, 'Say Amin [sic, "Amen"] when the Imam says it and if the Amin [sic] of any one of you coincides with that of the angels then all his past sins will be forgiven'" (Bukhari, 1:747).

The list of Muhammadan regulations regarding prayer is long and includes such things as not eating garlic (Bukhari, 1:815), bathing on Fridays (Bukhari, 2:2), keeping your hands off your hips (Bukhari, 2:310), and, as already mentioned, extra credit for those who arrive early (Bukhari, 2:51).

3. Zakat.

The Arabic origins of this term refers to "that which purifies." The Zakat is an obligatory tax that is used for charitable and other religious purposes. The precise determination of the amount to be assessed varies, but generally it consists of 2.5% of a Muslim's total income, savings, and wealth above a minimum level known as a "nisab." The tax is paid to Zakat collectors and then distributed to the poor, new converts, clergy, and those fighting for Islamic causes. The Zakat may only be spent on Muslims and to advance the cause of Islam.

Paradise holds special honors for those who practice the Five Pillars of Islam, including Zakat. "Allah's Apostle said, 'Whoever gives two kinds (of things or property) in charity for Allah's Cause, will be called from the gates of Paradise and will be addressed, 'O slaves of Allah! Here is prosperity'... whoever was amongst those who used to give in charity, will be called from the gate of charity" (Bukhari, 3:121).

Failure to pay the Zakat in full will result in punishment in the after-life. "The Prophet said, '(On the Day of Resurrection) camels will come to their owner in the best state of health they have ever had (in the world), and if he had not paid their Zakat (in the world) then they would tread him with their feet; and similarly, sheep will come to their owner in the best state of health they have ever had in the world, and if he had not paid their Zakat, then they would tread him with their hooves and would butt him with their horns'" (Bukhari, 2:485).

4. Hajj.

This word comes from the Arabic word meaning "to intend a journey" or "pilgrimage." Every adult Muslim is expected to make a pilgrimage to Mecca at least once in a lifetime as long as the person is physically and financially capable of making the journey and is able to support his family during the absence. The Hajj is conducted between the 8th and 12th (though sometimes the 13th) days of the last month in the Islamic calendar, Dhu al-Hijjah. Since Islam uses a lunar calendar, this date does not consistently correspond with specific dates in the western, or Georgian, calendar. Among other things, during the Hajj, pilgrims walk around the Kaaba seven times in a counter-clockwise direction and perform a symbolic stoning of the Devil by throwing rocks at three pillars.

5. Sawm.

"Sawm" is the Arabic word for fasting. Muslims are required to abstain from eating and drinking during the month of Ramadan. They also are expected to give up other pleasures like chewing gum, smoking, and conjugal sex. This fasting, however, is only done between sunrise and sunset. Muslims may eat and drink at night. There is another type of continuous fasting, but Muhammad prohibited anyone but himself from practicing it. Why? Because of his special status. "The Prophet said, 'Do not practice Al-Wisal (fasting continuously without breaking one's fast in the evening or eating before the following dawn).' The people said to the Prophet, 'But you practice Al-Wisal?' The Prophet replied, 'I am not like any of you, for I am given food and drink (by Allah) during the night'" (Bukhari, 3:182). "Who amongst you is similar to me?" (Bukhari, 3:186).

Muslims seek to grow in piety and nearness to God through this ritual abstinence. They also hope to become more empathetic with the less fortunate. Beyond this, "Allah's Apostle said... 'Fasting is a shield or protection from the fire and from committing sins" (Bukhari, 3:128). Of course, another powerful incentive is extra rewards in the afterlife. "The Prophet said, 'There is a gate in Paradise called

Ar-Raiyan, and those who observe fasts will enter through it on the Day of Resurrection and none except them will enter through it. It will be said, "Where are those who used to observe fasts?" They will get up, and none except them will enter through it. After their entry the gate will be closed and nobody will enter through it'" (Bukhari, 3:120).

CHAPTER EIGHT

THE SIXTH PILLAR OF ISLAM: JIHAD

"But the best death is on the battlefield" (Sira, 519).

The public face of Islam — the visage their marketing department wants you to see — is devout and compassionate. Fidelity, prayer, charity, pilgrimage, and fasting — there is nothing seemingly dangerous nor diabolical in these five pillars. But the public face of Islam is a lie — a mask which hides a sinister reality. It engages and distracts the uninformed with a warm smile while the sword is being drawn; and, make no mistake about it, it always has been the sword which does the real work of Islam. You see, there is a "Sixth Pillar" — one that outranks all the others except the first. It is this Sixth Pillar that truly defines Islam. It is this Sixth Pillar which has driven Islam and which explains the spread of Islam: Jihad.

The word "jihad" is often translated as "holy war," but that is not accurate. The Arabic word for "war" is "al-harb."

Jihad is really a "sacred struggle" which may or may not be violent. All Muslims are expected to participate however they can. Jihad can be carried out with the pen, the checkbook, and the lying tongue as well as with the sword. Still, jihad is ultimately executed violently.

Few things in Islam are honored as highly as jihad. It is the preeminent commission of Muhammad and Muslims. "Allah's Apostle said: 'I have been ordered (by Allah) to fight against the people until they testify that none has the right to be worshipped but Allah and that Muhammad is Allah's Apostle, and offer the prayers perfectly and give the obligatory charity, so if they perform that, then they save their lives and property from me except for Islamic laws and then their reckoning (accounts) will be done by Allah'" (Bukhari, 1:24). Notice, Muhammad has been ordered to fight, and the lives and property of others are only safe from confiscation if one accepts Islam. Other hadiths repeat the same sentiment, but the following one offers an additional detail which describes how vigorously Muhammad and his Muslims are expected to fight. "Allah's Apostle said, 'I have been ordered to fight the people till they say: "None has the right to be worshipped but Allah." And if they say so, pray like our prayers, face our Qibla [toward Mecca], and **slaughter as we slaughter**, then their blood and property will be sacred to us…" (Bukhari, 1:387, emphasis added). And "slaughter as we slaughter." Resistance cannot be tolerated. Opponents are to be subjugated by the butcher's blade.

I mentioned above that this Sixth Pillar outranks all the others in importance except the first. That wasn't an opinion. I was paraphrasing Muhammad. Now, allow me to quote him, "Allah's Apostle was asked, 'What is the best deed?' He replied, 'To believe in Allah and His Apostle (Muhammad).' The questioner then asked, 'What is the next (in goodness)?' He replied, 'To participate in Jihad (religious fighting) in Allah's Cause.' The questioner again asked, 'What is the next (in goodness)?' He replied, 'To perform Hajj (Pilgrimage to Mecca)…'" (Bukhari, 1:25). This was not the only time Muhammad expressed this conviction. "I asked the Prophet, 'What is the best deed?' He replied, 'To believe in Allah and to fight for His Cause'" (Bukhari, 3:694). Take note: Jihad is more important than all the other "pillars" except believing in Allah and his apostle. "The Prophet said, 'A single endeavor (of fighting) in Allah's Cause in the forenoon or in the afternoon is better than the world and whatever is in it'" (Bukhari, 4:50).

Jihad imparts a special glory and reward to all who participate; but in fact, all are expected to participate as best they can. Muhammad said, "Not equal are those believers who sit (at home) and those who strive hard and fight in the Cause of Allah with their wealth and lives" (Bukhari, 4:85). This same sentiment is found in the *Koran*: "Such believers as sit at home — unless they have an injury — are not the equals of those who struggle in the path of God with their possessions and their selves. God has preferred in rank those who struggle with their possessions and their selves over the ones who sit at home..." (*Koran*, 4:95). In fact, saying that god merely "prefers" those who participate in jihad to those who do not is putting it mildly. Very mildly. Consider the following. Muhammad said, "The man who dies without participating in jihad, who never desired to wage holy war, dies the death of a Hypocrite" (Muslim, 020, 4696). To a Muslim, the word "hypocrite" is a vile epithet. It is the same word used to describe a turncoat who abandons the Islamic faith. And now, consider this. Muhammad said, "Two angels descend from Paradise each day. One says, 'O, Allah! Reward those who contribute to jihad,' and the other says, 'O, Allah! Kill those who refuse to support jihad'" (Bukhari, 2,24,522).

To be sure, the reward for following the way of the jihadist is considerable. It is also mentioned repeatedly. "A man came to Allah's Apostle and said, 'Instruct me as to such a deed as equals Jihad (in reward).' He replied, 'I do not find such a deed.'... Abu-Huraira added, 'The Mujahid (i.e. Muslim fighter) is rewarded even for the footsteps of his horse while it wanders about (for grazing) tied in a long rope" (Bukhari 4:44). On another occasion, Muhammad said, "Allah promises that anyone killed while fighting for His cause will be admitted without question into Paradise. If such a holy warrior survives the battles, he can return home with the captured property and possessions of the defeated" (Bukhari, 4:52,46). Muhammad wanted to ensure that his warriors were well-motivated to give their all, so he often addressed the matter of reward, whether here on Earth or in Paradise, as we see in the following hadith. "The Prophet said, 'The person who participates in (Holy battles) in Allah's cause and nothing compels him to do so except belief in Allah and His Apostles, will be recompensed by Allah either with a reward, or booty (if he survives) or will be admitted to Paradise (if he is killed in the battle as a martyr)'" (Bukhari, 1:35). Islam even has a special term for the financial reward paid to those who participate in jihad. It is "Fai," or "war booty." Muhammad said, "'Whomever amongst us is killed will go to Paradise." Umar asked the Prophet. 'Is it not true that our men who are killed will go to Paradise and theirs (i.e. those of the Pagan's) will go to the (Hell) fire?' The Prophet said, 'Yes'" (Bukhari, 4:72).

As was mentioned above, jihad includes far more activities than those normally associated with warfare. Jihad is a sacred struggle that seeks to advance the cause of Islam. So, it should come as no surprise that the rewards of jihad are granted to all who participate in this sacred struggle, whether they bloody their hands directly or not. Muhammad said, "Anyone who arms a jihadist is rewarded just as a fighter would be; anyone who gives proper care to a holy warrior's dependents is rewarded just as a fighter would be" (Bukhari, 4:52,96).

Later in this book we will discuss the second-class status assigned to women in Islam. But make no mistake about it, their inferiority does not excuse them from participating in jihad. It just defines a different role. Muhammad's wife, Aisha, once asked, "'O Allah's Apostle!

We consider Jihad as the best deed. Should we not fight in Allah's Cause?' He said, 'The best Jihad (for women) is Hajj-Mabrur (i.e. Hajj which is done according to the Prophet's tradition and is accepted by Allah)'" (Bukhari, 4:43).

Glorification of Violence, Vengeance, and Death.

Islam is a religion literally dripping in blood, and it has created a culture that celebrates violence and death. But what else should be expected when god, himself, is a self-described terrorist? "When your Lord revealed to the angels: I am with you, therefore make firm those who believe. I will cast terror into the hearts of those who disbelieve. Therefore strike off their heads and strike off every fingertip of them" (*Koran*, 8:12). "When you meet the unbelievers, smite their necks [cut off their heads], then, when you have made wide slaughter among them, tie fast the bonds; then set them free, either by grace or ransom, till the war lays down its loads" (*Koran*, 47:4).

Savagery, brutality, and revenge are hallmarks of the Islamic creed. Consider the following accounts.

When asked what to do about a man who presumably was hiding loot from the Muslims, "the apostle gave orders to al-Zubayr b. al-Awwam, 'Torture him until you extract what he has,' so he kindled a fire with flint and steel on his chest until he was nearly dead. Then the apostle delivered him to Muhammad b. Maslama and he struck off his head in revenge for his brother Mahmud" (*Sira*, 763-764).

In the following narrative, one man, Muhayyisa, responds to Muhammad's decree to kill Jews by immediately murdering a Jew who had often aided him and his family. When Muhayyisa's brother, Huwayyisa, rebukes him, Muhayyisa responded by telling his brother that he would have killed him if Muhammad had so ordered. Huwayyisa found this "marvelous" and became a Muslim. Here is the actual account: "The apostle said, 'Kill any Jew that falls into your power.' Thereupon Muhayyisa b. Mas'ud leapt upon Ibn Sunayna, a Jewish merchant with whom they had social and business relations, and killed him" (*Sira*, 553). When Muhayyisa's brother heard about this he began to beat him, upset because their family had benefitted from their relationship with the Jewish merchant. "'You enemy of God, did you kill him when much of the fat on your belly comes from his wealth?' Muhayyisa answered, 'Had the one who ordered me to kill him ordered me to kill you I would have cut your head off.' He said that this was the beginning of Huwayyisa's [the brother's] acceptance of Islam. The other replied, 'By God, if Muhammad had ordered you to kill me would you have killed me?' He said, 'Yes, by God, had he ordered me to cut off your head I would have done so.' He exclaimed, 'By God, a religion which can bring you to this is marvelous!" and he became a Muslim" (*Sira*, 554).

Not only does Islam celebrate violence, violence and the threat of violence have always been the paramount recruiting tools for the Muslims. The *Koran* mandates that Kafirs first be given a chance to convert to Islam. If they accept the invitation, they are graciously welcomed into the fold and their indoctrination and assimilation begin. If the invitation is refused, they are not-so-graciously consigned to slavery or death. "Then, when the sacred months are drawn away, slay the idolaters wherever you find them, and take them, and confine them, and lie in wait for them at every place of ambush. But if they repent, and perform the prayer, and pay the alms, then let them go their way; God is All-forgiving, All-compassionate" (*Koran*, 9:5).

The following story is a good example of Islamic evangelism. "Then the apostle sent Khalid b. al-Walid in the month of Rabi'u' l-Akhir or Jumada'l-Ula in the year 10 [Islamic calendar] to the B. al-Harith b. Ka'b in Najran, and ordered him to invite them to Islam three days before he attacked them. If they accepted then he was to accept it from them; and if they declined he was to fight them. So Khalid sent out and came to them, and sent out riders in all directions inviting the people to Islam, saying, 'If you accept Islam you will be safe,' so the men accepted Islam as they were invited. Khalid stayed with them teaching them Islam and the book of God and the *sunna* of His prophet, for that was what the apostle of God had ordered him to do if they accepted Islam and did not fight" (Sira, 958-959). Here is a similar account. Umayr b. Wahb converted to Islam after originally being one of its persecutors in Mecca. He came to Muhammad in Medina with a special request. "'I used to be active in extinguishing the light of God and in persecuting those who followed God's religion. I should like you to give me permission to go to Mecca to summon them to God and His apostle and to Islam that perhaps God may guide them; and if not I will persecute them in their religion as I used to persecute your companions.' The apostle agreed and he went to Mecca" (*Sira*, 473).

Conversion, slavery, or death. Ultimately, these are the only options Islam recognizes for the Kafir. More on this later.

Martyrdom.

Not only is killing celebrated — so, too, is being killed if it is for Allah. The noblest death is that of the martyr. First, a technical note. Most definitions hold that a "martyr" is someone who dies for a cause, but the Muhammadan perspective is broader. "Then the Prophet said, 'Five are the martyrs: One who dies of plague, one who dies of an abdominal disease, one who dies of drowning, one who is buried alive (and) dies [from the collapse of a building] and one who is killed in Allah's cause'" (Bukhari, 1:624). However, the last category is the one most commonly associated with martyrdom and is the one we will consider here.

Muhammad expected his holy warriors to hold nothing back — to attack with a relentless ferocity that would terrorize and ultimately overwhelm all his enemies. However, it is no easy matter to motivate a person to overcome his greatest fear: namely, death. And so, Muhammad and his Muslims sought to inspire successive generations of jihadists with the promise of a reward so glorious that death itself would seem a paltry price to pay in order to achieve it. Employing a classic technique of any good brain-washer, Muhammad endlessly repeated accounts of the honor that would be awarded to the martyr. "Some men whom God **honored** with martyrdom..." (*Sira*, 558). "God **honored** several with martyrdom..." (*Sira*, 571). "perhaps God will **favor** him with martyrdom..." (*Sira*, 580). "God **honored** with martyrdom..." (*Sira*, 592).

Although Muhammad, himself, would be denied this honor, he often spoke as though he coveted it. Muhammad said, "By Him in Whose Hands my life is! I would love to be martyred in Allah's Cause and then get resurrected and then get martyred, and then get resurrected again and then get martyred and then get resurrected again and then get martyred" (Bukhari, 4:54). "The Prophet said, 'Nobody who enters Paradise likes to go back to the world even if he got everything on the earth, except a Mujahid [holy warrior] who wishes to return to the world so that he may be martyred ten times because of the dignity he receives (from Allah)'" (Bukhari, 4:72). "Amr b. Ubayd told me from al-Hasan that the apostle swore that there was no believer who had parted from the world and wanted to return to it for a single hour even if he could possess it with all it has except the martyr who would like to return and fight for God and be killed a second time" (*Sira*, 606).

Apparently, Muhammad's enthusiasm for a divine death was contagious. One convert confessed that, "What led me to become a Muslim was that I stabbed one of them between the shoulders that day and I saw the point of the spear come out of his chest, and I heard him say, 'I have won by God!' I could not make out what he meant by the words seeing that I had killed him until afterwards I asked others and was told that it was martyrdom, and then I said, 'By God he has won" (*Sira*, 650). A man named Urwa b. Masud al-Thaqafi converted to Islam and returned to his people to convince them to convert as well. He told this story about a Muslim warrior who was killed in battle. "[T]hey shot arrows at him from all directions, and one hit him and killed him." Before dying, one of his attackers asked him, "'What do you think about your death?' He said, 'It is a gift which God has honored me with and a martyrdom which God has led me to'" (*Sira*, 914). Muhammad's successors continued to carry the banner of martyrdom. "Umar [the second caliph after Muhammad] said, 'O Allah! Grant me martyrdom in Your cause, and let my death be in the city of Your Apostle'" (Bukhari, 3:114).

This enthusiasm for self-sacrifice has continued to the present age. Scarcely a day goes by that we don't hear or read about the devastation wrought by some suicidal jihadist. Actually, the term "suicide bomber" or "suicidal jihadist" is not accurate from an Islamic perspective. Suicide is forbidden in Islam, but killing oneself while attempting to kill Kafirs is not considered suicide. It is a glorious act of martyrdom and a ticket straight to Paradise. "Allah's Apostle said, 'Know that Paradise is under the shades of swords'" (Bukhari, 4:73).

Now, it is true that Jews and Christians also honor those who die for God. "Precious in the sight of the Lord is the death of His saints" (Psalm 116:15). But whereas Christians and Jews commemorate and venerate, Muslims celebrate and revel. To a Jew or Christian, the death of a martyr is deeply respected but also deeply regretted. To Muhammad and his followers, it is something to relish.

Jihad is Deceit.

In the *Bible*, the Eighth or Ninth Commandment, depending on which numbering system you prefer, states that one should not bear false witness (Exodus 20:16). Most theologians agree that this prohibition against making deliberately false statements is not limited to courtroom appearances, as the word "witness" may suggest to the modern ear. It is a broad condemnation of lying in general. It is a broad condemnation which Islam does not recognize. As we shall examine in more detail in the chapter on Islamic dualism, lying, in itself, is neither good nor bad. The morality or immorality of the act all depends upon who is doing the lying and to whom one is lying. Lying to a Muslim is generally bad — not always, but generally. Lying to a Kafir in order to advance the cause of Islam is good. The Muslims even have a special word for righteous deceit or "sacred deception," which is practiced against Kafirs. The word is "taqiyya." For example, the leader of a rabidly jihadist nation could promise that he has absolutely no intentions of sponsoring terrorism against non-Islamic peoples or of acquiring weapons of mass destruction all the while he is actively engaged in both pursuits. This is "Taqiyya," and it is perfectly acceptable — in fact, it is encouraged if it advances the cause of Islam. Another form of permissible lying is "kitman," which allows telling a partial truth. For example, an imam or mullah can assure all us Kafirs that Islam is a "peaceful" religion, while conveniently leaving out the part that, to a Muslim, "peace" refers to all things which work to the benefit of Islam. With this perspective, flying airliners into tall buildings, beheading helpless captives, and blowing up oneself in a crowded marketplace or school yard is actually "peaceful" if it is perceived as advancing the cause of Islam.

There is an interesting passage in the *Koran* which underscores the permissibility of lying if it furthers Allah's cause. Like many other passages in the *Koran*, it is difficult to follow, and the point about deceit is easy to miss. Still, it will be worth our while to take a moment to examine it here. "Whoso disbelieves in God, after he has believed — excepting him who has been compelled, and his heart is still at rest in his belief — but whosoever's breast is expanded in unbelief, upon them shall rest anger from God, and there awaits them a mighty chastisement…" (*Koran*, 16:106). The main thrust of the passage is that a "mighty chastisement" awaits those who once came to believe in Islam but then left the faith. However, the passage which says "excepting him who has been compelled, and his heart is still at rest in his belief" allows Muslims to lie about being Muslim if he feels compelled to do so for the advancement of Islam and as long as he remains faithful at heart. This is still another example of "Taqiyya" — sacred deception.

Now, if we put together what we have just learned about "taqiyya," "kitman," and verse 16:106 from the *Koran*, we begin to realize how difficult it is for Kafirs to deal confidently with Muslims at any level; from buying a car, to taking an oath to "preserve, protect, and defend the Constitution," to negotiating a peace agreement. They will lie to your face and feel good about it. And it is all sanctioned from on high. "Muhammad cried out, 'Jihad is deceit'" (Bukhari,4:52,267). "Allah's Apostle called, 'War is deceit'" (Bukhari, 4:268). "The Prophet said, 'War is deceit'" (Bukhari 4:269).

CHAPTER NINE

ISLAMIC DUALISM: THE WORST OF BOTH WORLDS

Judeo-Christian tenets teach that certain deeds are good and certain deeds are bad. Period. The Decalogue, or Ten Commandments, states unequivocally that "thou shalt" honor the sabbath and your parents. On the other hand, it declares that "thou shalt not" have other gods, make graven images of false gods, use God's Name in vain, murder, commit adultery, steal, bear false witness, or covet. There are no asterisks nor footnotes attached to attenuate nor qualify these statements. Right is right. Wrong is wrong. Furthermore, these principles apply whether or not a person is dealing with someone who shares his religious views. Morality is uniform and universal.

This is not true of Islam. Islam does not hold that there is one universal code of conduct that applies to everyone and in all circumstances. A particular deed is not necessarily good nor bad simply because "it is." Circumstances dictate morality; and the preeminent determining circumstance is the religion of the person with whom one is dealing. In short, there is one code of conduct for Muslims dealing with other Muslims and a different code of conduct for Muslims dealing with nonbelievers, or Kafirs. This "duality" is a key element of "Islamic morality"; and it is an element that all non-believers must keep in mind when dealing with Muslims.

Jesus taught, "So in everything, do to others what you would have them do to you, for this sums up the Law and the Prophets" (Matthew 7:12, NIV). This passage is commonly known as the "Golden Rule," and it says simply that each of us should treat others the way we want to be treated. Muhammad had a "Golden Rule" of his own; but as you will see, his was not nearly as universal and inclusive as the one that Jesus taught. "The Prophet said, 'None of you will have faith till he wishes for his (Muslim) brother what he likes for himself'" (Bukhari, 1:12). By the way, I did not add the word "Muslim" in parentheses. It is from the original text, as I explained in my opening comments. In short, Jesus taught that each one should treat everyone the way he wants to be treated. Muhammad taught that each Muslim should treat other Muslims the way he wants to be treated. Kafirs? Well, that's a different matter. Whereas there isn't much that a Muslim shouldn't do **for** a brother Muslim, there isn't much a Muslim cannot do **to** a non-believer — including lying, robbing, raping, kidnapping, imprisonment, enslavement, torture, and murder — as was demonstrated in the behavior of the model Muslim Muhammad himself, which we saw in his brief biography.

The justification for this is simple: "God loveth not the unbelievers" (*Sira*, 406). As for "those who disbelieve — for them awaits a draught of boiling water, and a painful chastisement, for their disbelieving" (*Koran*, 10:4). Whereas the God of the *Bible* loved all people so much that He sacrificed His "only begotten Son" to save them, the god of the *Koran* decreed that "those who fight against God and His Messenger... shall be slaughtered, or crucified, or their hands and feet shall alternately be struck off, or they shall be banished from the land" (*Koran*, 5:33). It is true that the Jehovah of the Old Testament often warned of dire consequences that would come to those who did not obey him; but these dire consequences resulted from removing oneself from God's protection. Allah, on the other hand, is a ravenous beast who goes gunning for those who dare to deny and defy him. And since Muhammad and his Muslims were the agents of this ravenous beast, they, too, could employ similar tactics.

The conditional morality of Islam has long proved to be a powerful weapon in the hands of Muslims. Unrestrained by the limitations of a universal moral code, Muslims are basically free to do whatever they want so long as they can claim that it is in the interests of serving Allah. How very convenient. Of course, it is a convenience that they learned from their master, who was not at all shy about claiming for himself special dispensations in order to do what he wanted, when he wanted, and in the way he wanted, even if it was contrary to traditional practices and mores. Whether taking wives or taking lives, Allah proved an indulgent lord when Muhammad's desires were at issue. Consider the following.

Muhammad became convinced that members of a certain Jewish community had partaken in a conspiracy to kill him. "The apostle ordered them [his followers] to prepare for war and to march against them [the Jews]. Then he went off with the men until he came upon them. The Jews took refuge in their forts and the apostle ordered that the palm-trees should be cut down and burnt, and they called out to him, 'Muhammad, you have prohibited wanton destruction and blamed those guilty of it. Why then are you cutting down and burning our palm-trees?'" (*Sira*, 653). Understand that people who live in the desert cherish their trees — especially those that bear fruit, like the date palm. The fruit of the date palm was a key element in the diet and economies of these people. The wanton destruction of trees like this was considered a "crime against humanity," and something which Muhammad, himself, had criticized. But now, Muhammad saw it to be in his interests to cut down and burn the trees, and he was called on it. So, how did Muhammad answer the accusation? "'It was by God's permission,' i.e. they were cut done by God's order; it was not destruction but was vengeance from God, 'and to humble evil-doers" (*Sira*, 654). Islamic duality.

After Muhammad's triumphal return to Mecca, he ordered a number of his old enemies to be killed. Some complained that it was not lawful to kill inside the holy city of Mecca. Once again, Muhammad claimed a special dispensation from Allah allowing him to do what others could not. "The apostle arose and addressed us, saying, 'God made Mecca holy the day He created heaven and earth, and it is the holy of holies until the resurrection day. It is not lawful for anyone who believes in God and the last day to shed blood therein, nor to cut down trees therein. It was not lawful to anyone before me and it will not be lawful to anyone after me. Indeed, it is not lawful for me except at this time because of (God's) anger against its people. Now it has regained its former holiness. Let those here now tell those that are not here. If anyone should say, 'The apostle killed men in Mecca', say God permitted His apostle to do so but He does not permit you" (*Sira*, 823-824). Islamic duality.

From the time that Muhammad moved to Medina, thievery became an important part of Muslim economics. It is how Muhammad funded his jihad and how he lured his mujahid, or holy warriors, to join the cause and remain faithful. Inconveniently, taking plunder was generally considered illegal and immoral even back in Muhammad's time; but, as you may have guessed, Muhammad received another special dispensation on the matter. Muhammad said, "The booty has been made Halal (lawful) for me yet it was not lawful for anyone else before me." In other words, "Thou shall not steal," unless you happen to be Muhammad. Islamic duality.

We have already discussed another area where conventional mores were shelved in order to suit Muhammad's desires: the taking of wives. Whereas the *Koran* honors the custom of having up to four wives (*Koran*, 4:3), Muhammad had thirteen, and apparently as many as nine at the same time. Islamic duality.

Ironically, one of the clearest examples of Islamic duality, or hypocrisy, is revealed in Muhammad's own pronouncement against hypocrites. "The Prophet said, 'The signs of a hypocrite are three: 1. Whenever he speaks, he tells a lie. 2. Whenever he promises, he always breaks it (his promise). 3. If you trust him, he proves to be dishonest'" (Bukhari, 1:32). And yet, all three of the above — lying, breaking promises, and being untrustworthy — are permissible when dealing with Kafirs. We already have discussed "taqiyya" (sacred deceit) and "kitman" (telling a partial truth). Deception which aids Islam is not only permissible, it is noble. Remember, "Jihad is deceit."

The following is an account that shows Muhammad approving the use of lies to accomplish his objective. When an unbeliever wrote insulting verses about Muslim women, Muhammad asked, "'Who will rid me of Ibnu'l-Ashraf?' Muhammad b. Maslama, brother of the B. Abdu'l-Ashhal, said, 'I will deal with him for you, O apostle of God, I will kill him.' He said, 'Do so if you can.'" The would-be assassin began planning the murder, but his scheme involved deceit, which he feared might offend Allah. He told Muhammad, "'O apostle of God, we shall have to tell lies.' He answered, 'Say what you like, for you are free in the matter'" (*Sira*, 550). The plan worked and the deceit was celebrated in a poem that included the line, "He beguiled him and brought him down with guile…" (*Sira*, 553).

Yes, there are two codes of conduct in the Islamic world: the one you apply to fellow Muslims and the one you apply to the Kafirs. Our international negotiators would be well-advised to remember this. Muslims are always expected to be relentless in their pursuit of victory against the Kafirs. Allah said, "O you who believe, when you meet those who disbelieve on the march, do not turn your backs. He who turns his back except in maneuvering or intending to join another section, incurs the wrath of God, and his destination is Hell, a miserable end" (*Sira*, 477). The only time it is acceptable to negotiate with Kafirs and Kafir nations is when the Muslim side is at a disadvantage; and then it is required that the agreement be broken as soon as it suits the interests of Islam. Integrity simply is not a consideration when dealing with the non-believer.

Islam: Religion of Peace.

One of the most glaring examples of Islamic duality is the claim that Islam is a religion of peace. The words and the deeds of Muslims seem to race in opposite directions — at least to the untrained eye. But, once again, there is a special, twisted logic within Islam that reconciles the apparent discrepancy — at least, if you have a bent for twisted logic.

Despite the blood that still drips from Muhammad's sword, despite the rivers of blood that flow from the pages of the history books and today's newspapers, we still hear the imams, the mullahs, and their "useful idiots" (as Lenin put it) proclaim that Islam is a peaceful religion. They claim that Islam only fights against those who fight it first. To support that claim, they quote Koranic verses like the following: "And fight in the way of God with those who fight with you, but aggress not: God loves not the aggressors. And slay them wherever you come upon them, and expel them from where they expelled you; persecution is more grievous than slaying. But fight them not by the Holy Mosque until they should fight you there; then, if they fight you, slay them — such is the recompense of unbelievers — but if they give over, surely God is All-forgiving, All-compassionate. Fight them, till there is no persecution and the religion is God's; then if they give over, there shall be no enmity save for evildoers" (*Koran*, 2:190-193).

In short, the *Koran* admonishes Muslims that they should not fight unless they are first attacked. Do not be the aggressor. God does not love the aggressor. That sounds pretty reasonable; but it almost certainly will be misinterpreted unless one accurately understands the Islamic mindset. Remember, their goal is to convert the world. "Fight them, until there is no persecution and the religion is God's..." (*Koran*, 2:193). When a Muslim encounters a non-believer, he first must offer the option to convert. Should the non-believer refuse the offer, he already has committed an act of aggression against Allah, and the Muslim is free to respond — to fight "with those who fight with you." You see, in their mind, we Kafirs started the fight as soon as we turned down their kind offer to convert. Enslaving school girls, beheading journalists, immolating captives, drowning prisoners, crucifying infidels, bombing marketplaces, shooting up newspapers, butchering critics, and toppling skyscrapers are all justified responses to the "aggression" of others; but these are not acts of aggression themselves. Jihad is considered defensive.

Those who argue that Islam is a peaceful religion either have been duped or are doing the duping. Consider these blunt words of the Ayatollah Khomeini: "Those who know nothing of Islam pretend that Islam counsels against war. Those (who say this) are witless. Islam says: Kill all the unbelievers just as they would kill you all! Does this mean that Muslims should sit back until they are devoured by (the unbelievers)? Islam says: Kill them, put them to the sword and scatter (their armies).... Islam says: Whatever good there is exists thanks to the sword and in the shadow of the sword! People cannot be made obedient except with the sword! The sword is the key to Paradise, which can be opened only to the Holy Warriors! There are hundreds of other (Quranic) psalms and Hadiths (sayings of the Prophet) urging Muslims to value war and to fight. Does all this mean that Islam is a religion that prevents men from waging war? I spit upon those foolish souls who make such a claim" (Amir Taheri, *Holy Terror: Inside the World of Islamic Terrorism*, New York: Alder & Alder, 1987, p. 241-43).

On December 2, 2015, the worst terrorist attack on American soil since 911 took place in my home town, San Bernardino, California. Fourteen were killed and twenty-two wounded. About two weeks before the horrific event, Syed Farook, a Muslim and one of the shooters, was engaged in a heated debate with a co-worker, Nicholas Thalasinos. Ironically, the debate was about whether or not Islam was a peaceful religion. Farook argued passionately that Islam is peaceful. Two weeks later he mercilessly slaughtered fourteen people, including Thalasinos. That is Islamic peace. That is how Muslims win arguments. They kill the opposition.

Religion of peace? It all depends on how you define "peace." Islamic "peace" will only come when all the peoples of the earth become Muslims and followers of Allah. Until then, the Muslim must fight to convert, enslave, or kill the Kafirs. These are the only three options available for the non-believer.

* * *

Kab b. Malik was inspired to write these verses after observing one of the Muslim raids following the fall of Mecca:

"We shall fight as long as we live
Till you turn to Islam, humbly seeking refuge.
We will fight not caring whom we meet
Whether we destroy ancient holdings or
newly gotten gains.

How many tribes assembled against us
Their finest stock and allies!
They came at us thinking they had no equal
And we cut off their noses and ears
With our fine polished Indian swords,
Driving them violently before us
To the command of God and Islam.
Until religion is established, just and straight, and
Al-Lat and al-Uzza and Wudd are forgotten
And we plunder them of their necklaces and earrings.
For they had become established and confident,
And he who cannot protect himself must suffer
disgrace" (*Sira*, 871).

Nothing has changed. "Do not faint and call for peace…"
(*Koran*, 47:35).

A Gang with a God.

Violence, theft, assault, swarming, mutilation, murder, intimidation, extortion, vandalism, vengeance,
trafficking in illegal and immoral activities, rituals, ter-
ritoriality, extreme bigotry toward outsiders, one-way
membership (once you're in, you stay in), and authoritative, charismatic, dictatorial leadership. I just listed
many of the salient characteristics which define a gang.
The reader may have thought that I was summarizing
the ideology and practice of Islam, as we have read
from the pages of its own writings. Well, yes, I did that,

too. You see, what Muhammad did was create a seventh century gang — with a twist. He added a new element. He gave it a god, and this supercharged his gang. By throwing god into the mix, he legitimized all the most vicious and carnal instincts of man and granted his followers license to fulfill their most loathsome, reprehensible, and vile fantasies — as long as they did these things to outsiders — the Kafirs. His Muslims made the Cosa Nostra, Wah Ching, Bloods, Crips, Yakuza, Los Zetas, and MS-13 look like altar boys by comparison. He masterfully blended the power of our darkest desires with the zealousness that comes from believing one is serving god. The result was the fanatical syndicate that changed history and threatens the world to this day. Islam is a gang with a god. Remember this when the time comes in a few chapters to consider our response to Islam.

CHAPTER TEN

WOMEN

Throughout history, women often have been regarded as inferior and subservient. They frequently have been treated as chattel, and even disposable. Thankfully, these attitudes have changed in many modern-day cultures. Islam does not happen to be one of them. Muhammad's callous attitude about females continues unabated. The burqa, hijab, and niqab are merely external manifestations of a deeply entrenched and inveterate disdain for women within Islam. Women are generally held to be less intelligent than men, less righteous, less trustworthy, and less deserving of reward. They often have been reduced to the status of property and plunder even by Muhammad himself — and always with Allah's blessings. We will now turn to Islamic scripture to verify these assertions.

First, it must be acknowledged that Islamic doctrine is not utterly anti-female. Motherhood is revered; but other than that, there is only one time when men and women will be considered equal — on Judgment Day. "And whosoever does deeds of righteousness, be it male or female, believing — they shall enter Paradise, and not be wronged a single date-spot [treated unfairly]" (*Koran*, 4:124).

Women are to be subservient to men who may beat them if they rebel. "Men are the managers of the affairs of women for that God has preferred in bounty one of them over another, and for that they have expended of their property. Righteous women are therefore obedient, guarding the secret for God's guarding. And those you fear maybe rebellious admonish; banish them to their couches, and beat them." (*Koran*, 4:34)

Women are often described and treated as property. In the following quote from the *Koran*, Allah — through Muhammad — compares women to a field to be plowed and used as the farmer chooses. "Your women are a tillage for you; so come unto your tillage as you wish..." (*Koran*, 2:223).

Islam's disrespect for women can be seen easily in the way Muhammad and other Muslims treated captives. Muhammad's disparaging and dismissive attitude toward women, as well as his self-serving conditional morality, are both clearly illustrated in the following passage. "We conquered Khaibar [also "Khaybar"], took the captives, and the booty was collected. Dihya came and said, 'O Allah's Prophet! Give me a slave girl from the captives.' The Prophet said, 'Go and take any slave girl.' He took Safiya bint Huyai. A man came to the Prophet and said, 'O Allah's Apostles! [sic, should be "Apostle"] You gave Safiya bint Huyai to Dihya and she is the chief mistress of the tribes of Quraiza and An-Nadir and she befits none but you.' So the Prophet said, 'Bring him along with her.' So Dihya came with her and when the Prophet saw her, he said to Dihya, 'Take any slave girl other than her from the captives.' Anas added: The Prophet then manumitted [freed] her and married her" (Bukhari, 1:367). Rank has its privileges.

In the following account from the *Sira* entitled, "Division of the Spoil of Hawazin and Gifts to Gain Men's Hearts," we see how Muhammad doles out captured girls to his Companions much like the owner of a bakery would hand out free donuts to his friends. The story relates how "the apostle gave Ali a girl called Rayta d. Hilal b. Hayyan b. Umayra b. Hilal b. Nasira b. Qusayya b. Nasr b. Sad b. Bakr; and he gave Uthman a girl called Zaynab d. Hayyan; and he gave Umar a girl whom Umar gave to his son Abdullah" (*Sira*, 878).

Islamic marriage is far from an equal partnership. To be sure, Muhammad spoke of the rights a wife has over her husband; but as you will soon read, these "rights" sound more like a slave's remuneration than an equal's entitlement. During a hajj to Mecca, Muhammad "made a speech in which he made things clear" (*Sira*, 968). In that speech he said, "You have rights over your wives and they have rights over you. You have the right that they should not defile your bed and that they should not behave with open unseemliness. If they do, God allows you to put them in separate rooms and to beat them not with severity. If they refrain from these things they have the right to their food and clothing with kindness. Lay injunctions on women kindly, for they are prisoners with you having no control of their persons. You have taken them only as a trust from God, and you have the enjoyment of their persons by the words of God, so understand my words, O men, for I have told you" (*Sira*, 969).

It bears repetition that Muhammad described wives as their husbands' "prisoners" and that these prisoners have "no control of their persons." The preeminence of a husband's rights over his wives was further illuminated by one of Muhammad's "Companions" or closest associates, when he was asked by a woman on a trip to Yaman, "'O companion of God's apostle, what rights has a husband over his wife?' He said, 'Woe to you, a woman can never fulfill her husband's rights, so do your utmost to fulfill his claims as best you can.' She said, 'By God, if you are the companion of God's apostle you must know what rights a husband has over his wife?' He said, 'If you were to go back and find him with his nostrils running with pus and blood and sucked until you got rid of them you would not have fulfilled your obligation'" (*Sira*, 957).

If a wife were ever so bold as to shun her husband's amorous advances, she could be beaten for being rebellious; but even if the husband should treat her more mercifully, god will not. "Allah's Apostle said, 'If a husband calls his wife to his bed (i.e. to have sexual relation) and she refuses and causes him to sleep in anger, the angels will curse her till morning'" (Bukhari, 4:460).

Some of the qualities which define a good wife are described in verse 5 of the *Koran's* 66th Sura. These traits include "women who have surrendered" and are "believing, obedient, penitent, devout, given to fasting... and virgins too."

Another shameful element of Islamic marriage customs has to do with the continuing practice of child marriage, which is approved by Allah and was indulged in by Muhammad. The 65th Sura of the *Koran* discusses rules for divorce. It prescribes a waiting period to determine if a wife is pregnant before divorcing her. "If you are in doubt concerning those of your wives who have ceased menstruating, know that their waiting period shall be three months. The same shall apply to those who have not yet menstruated" (*Koran*, 65:4). Wives "who have not yet menstruated" would be pre-pubescent. This raises the question, just how pre-pubescent can a wife be? Well, remember that Muhammad is the model, and he "married Aisha when she was a girl of six years of age, and he consummated that marriage when she was nine years old" (Bukhari, 5:63;3896). A different hadith (Hisham, 918) claims Aisha was seven when she married Muhammad and nine or ten when the marriage was consummated, but what's a year among friends? Modern apologists may try to dismiss this as merely the custom of a different time. Whereas it is true that many ancient cultures allowed females to marry at a much younger age than is considered appropriate now, "deflowering" a nine-year-old is an obscenity in any era. And as for the argument that it applied to Muslims of a "different time," well, maybe not. Iran's Ayatollah Khomeini called it a "divine blessing" to marry a girl before she began menstruating. He advised fathers, "Do your best to ensure that your daughters do not see their first blood in your house" (Amir Taheri, *The Spirit of Allah: Khomeini and the Islamic Revolution;* New York, Adler and Adler, 1986,90-91).

Women are considered to be both intellectually and spiritually inferior to men. "The Prophet said: 'I was shown the Hell-fire and that the majority of its dwellers were women who were ungrateful.' It was asked, 'Do they disbelieve in Allah' (or are they ungrateful to Allah)? He replied, 'They are ungrateful to their husbands and are ungrateful for the favors and the good (charitable deeds) done to them" (Bukhari, 1:28). The Prophet elaborated on this statement elsewhere. One day, on the way to offer prayer, Muhammad "passed by the women and said, 'O women! Give alms, as I have seen that the majority of the dwellers of Hell-fire were you (women).' Then they asked, 'Why is it so, O Allah's Apostle?' He replied, 'You curse frequently and are ungrateful to your husbands. I have not seen anyone more deficient in intelligence and religion than you. A cautious sensible man could be led astray by some of you.' The women asked, 'O Allah's Apostle! What is deficient in our intelligence and religion?' He said, 'Is not the evidence of two women equal to the witness of one man?' They replied in the affirmative. He said, 'This is the deficiency in her intelligence. Isn't it true that a woman can neither pray nor fast during her menses?' The women replied in the affirmative. He said, 'This is the deficiency in her religion'" (Bukhari, 1:301). Elsewhere, "The Prophet said, 'Isn't the witness of a woman equal to half of that of a man?' The women said, 'Yes.' He said, 'This is because of the deficiency of a woman's mind'" (Bukhari, 3:826). The "deficiency" associated with a woman's menstruation was also repeated elsewhere. "The Prophet said, 'Isn't it true that a woman does not pray and does not fast on menstruating? And that is the defect (a loss) in her religion'" (Bukhari, 3:172).

Here we see Muhammad degrading women because of the cultural biases imposed upon them, not because of any inherent deficiency of the women themselves. Cultural tradition and the *Koran* maintained that it took the testimony of two women to equal that of one man. ("And call in to witness two witnesses, men; or if the two be not men, then one man and two women, such witnesses as you approve of, that if one of the two women errs the other will remind her..." (*Koran*, 2:282). Muhammad then proceeded to use this arbitrary custom as evidence that women are intellectually inferior. He used another arbitrary practice — namely, that a woman should neither pray nor fast during menstruation — as evidence of her spiritual inferiority. It would make about as much sense to mandate that those who have facial hair (men) cannot pray nor fast and, therefore, they are spiritually inferior.

The teachings of Allah's messenger also make it clear that the most righteous and first entrants to Paradise will be men. "Allah's Apostle said, 'The first group (of people) who will enter Paradise will be (glittering) like the moon when it is full. They will not spit or blow their noses or relieve nature. Their utensils will be of gold and their combs of gold and silver; in their centers the aloe wood will be used, and their sweat will smell like musk. Everyone of them will have two wives; the marrow of the bones of the wives' legs will be seen through the flesh out of excessive beauty'" (Bukhari, 4:468). Elsewhere, Muhammad claimed that among these first entrants into Paradise, "everyone will have two wives from the houris, (who will be so beautiful, pure and transparent that) the marrow of the bones of their legs will be seen through the bones and the flesh." "Houris" were women of especial beauty. Notice the male orientation. If those who enter Paradise first have two wives, they can't be women. True, they will bring women with them, but these are trophy wives in the truest sense. The houris will be prizes awarded to the most righteous, who will be men. As an interesting side note, I never found a hadith indicating that any women in Paradise will have two husbands. Perhaps that wouldn't be much of a prize.

We see the "Fifty Percent Rule" show up in other areas of Islamic culture as well. Not only is the testimony of a woman worth half as much as that of a man, she is also entitled to only half as much inheritance. "Allah thus directs you as regards your children's inheritance: to the male, a portion equal to that of two females…" (*Koran*, 4:11). "Then Allah cancelled from that custom whatever He wished and fixed for the male double the amount inherited by the female…" (Bukhari, 4:10).

If women are due less rewards than men, wouldn't it be consistent with Islamic logic to expect that they they also would be due more punishment? Yep, they are. Here is an example: "Allah's Apostle ordered that an un-married man who committed illegal sexual intercourse be scourged one hundred lashes and sent into exile for one year" (Bukhari, 3:817). The man's female partner was stoned to death. Here's the more detailed story. "A bed-ouin came and said, 'O Allah's Apostle! Judge between us according to Allah's Laws... My son was a laborer working for this man, and he committed illegal sexual intercourse with his wife'... 'The Prophet said, "No doubt I will judge between you according to Allah's Law... your son will get a hundred lashes and one year exile... O Unais! go to the wife of this (man) and stone her to death.' So, Unais went and stoned her to death" (Bukhari, 3:860). The man got a spanking and a time-out. The woman was executed.

Considering the Islamic view of women, it should come as no surprise to see how many areas of their lives are strictly regulated by the men who dominate them. Most of us are already familiar with the restrictive dress code imposed on women. Muhammad commanded that, "When a woman reaches the age of menstruation, it does not suit her that she displays her parts of body except...face and hands" (Abu Dawud, 32:4092). But the restrictions do not end there. Consider the following mandates concerning travel and mourning: "The Prophet said, 'A woman should not travel for more than three days except with a Dhi-Mahram (i.e. a male with whom she cannot marry at all, e.g. her brother, father, grandfather, etc.) or her own husband" (Bukhari, 2:192). Elsewhere, Muhammad is quoted as saying that the time limit is "one day and night" (Bukhari, 2:194), or "two days" (Bukhari, 3:215). Muhammad also declared, "It is not legal for a woman who believes in Allah and the Last Day to mourn for more than three days for any dead person except her husband, for whom she should mourn for four months and ten days" (Bukhari, 2:370).

Earlier we discussed the supreme importance of participating in jihad. Women are also expected to do their share; but, once again, their share is different from that of a man. Aisha, one of Muhammad's wives, once asked, "'O Allah's Apostle! We consider Jihad as the best deed. Should we not fight in Allah's Cause?' He said, 'The best Jihad (for women) is Hajj-Mabrur (i.e. Hajj which is done according to the Prophet's tradition and is accepted by Allah)'" (Bukhari, 4:43). The best jihad for women is hajj, but that is not as good as the jihad reserved for men: "But the best death is on the battlefield" (*Sira*, 519).

Apparently, the vile nature of women is so great that they are even capable of negating the power of prayer. Aisha also passed on this proclamation, which is repeated in several other hadiths: "The things which annul the prayers were mentioned before me. They said, 'Prayer is annulled by a dog, a donkey and a woman (if they pass in front of the praying people)'" (Bukhari, 1:490).

If a woman's depravity is so great that she can cancel out the effectiveness of prayer, you certainly would not want to have one in leadership positions. Actually, that is no mere speculation. Muhammad clearly asserted his view that women make poor national leaders. "During the battle of Al-Jamal, Muhammad heard the news that the people of Persia had made the daughter of Khosrau their ruler. On this, he said, "A nation that makes a woman their ruler will never succeed" (Bukhari, 9:88,219).

The persecution of women is the shame of many ancient cultures and some modern ones. A "War on Women" continues to some degree in many places around the globe; but among Islamic nations, that "war" has taken on the proportions of jihad. When descending into the Islamic culture, one will see the clock spin backward, hear the clanking of chains, and smell the stench of persecution — especially for women.

CHAPTER ELEVEN

KAFIRS

The term "Kafir" comes from an Arabic word that means "deny." A "Kafir," therefore, is one who "denies" the "truth" of Islam. The Arabic word is usually translated as "non-believer" or "infidel." This translation is reasonably accurate, if one were merely to consider the word's denotation. However, "Kafir" has a strong pejorative connotation, and so the word is actually a vile slur referring to any non-Muslim. In short, a Kafir is anyone who does not accept Allah as the one, true god and Muhammad as his prophet. For this reason, they deserve the utmost contempt.

As was discussed earlier, there is a moral duality that is inextricably woven into Islam. Nowhere is this duality more clearly expressed than in the distinction between Muslims and Kafirs. Allah does **not** love all mankind — only Muslims. Islam has no "Golden Rule," at least as it is understood in Christian theology. Many of the verses quoted from the *Koran* by Islamic apologists to portray the religion as loving, compassionate, and peaceful only apply to Muslims. Whereas there isn't much a Muslim shouldn't do **for** a fellow believer, there isn't much a Muslim shouldn't do **to** a Kafir — including lying, robbing, raping, enslaving, torturing, killing, and completely annihilating their culture and religion. Remember, Muhammad is the exemplar — the perfect model to be emulated — and Muhammad enthusiastically did all of these things to Kafirs.

The moral duality of Islam is seen very clearly in what many people regard as the greatest of crimes and sins: murder. Generally speaking, it is a capital offense for one Muslim to murder another. The same is not true should a Muslim kill a Kafir. One of Muhammad's closest companions and one of his successors, Ali, confirmed "the judgment that no Muslim should be killed for killing an infidel" (Bukhari, 4:283).

The *Koran* contains over two dozen verses attesting that Allah does not love Kafirs. The *Sira* and hadiths faithfully follow suit. "God has cursed the unbelievers, and prepared for them a Blaze, therein to dwell for ever; they shall find neither protector nor helper" (*Koran*, 33:64-5). "Whosoever is an enemy to God and His angels and His Messengers, and Gabriel, and Michael — surely God is an enemy to the unbelievers" (*Koran*, 2:98). "As for the unbelievers, alike it is to them whether thou hast warned them or hast not warned them, they do not believe. God has set a seal on their hearts and on their hearing, and on their eyes is a covering, and there awaits them a mighty chastisement" (*Koran*, 2:6-7). "When thy Lord was revealing to the angels, 'I am with you; so confirm the believers. I shall cast into the unbelievers' hearts terror; so smite above the necks, and smite every finger of them!' That, because they had made a breach with God and with His Messenger; and whosoever makes a breach with God and with His messenger, surely God is terrible in retribution. That for you; therefore taste it; and that the chastisement of the Fire is for the unbelievers" (*Koran*, 8:12-14). "God loveth not the unbelievers" (*Sira*, 406). "[T]he unbelievers are for you a manifest foe" (*Koran*, 4:101).

Kafirs are not merely wretched, misguided souls. They are the "manifest foe," and Muslims are to treat them as such. The only acceptable relationship with a Kafir is Jihad, or "sacred struggle." "Coexist" is not part of the Islamic lexicon, except as a ploy to deceive the Kafir. And the Muslim should never shy away from extreme tactics. Muhammad didn't, as we have seen. In a sura entitled, "Muhammad" it states, "When you meet the unbelievers [Kafirs] smite their necks [cut off their heads], then, when you have made wide slaughter among them, tie fast the bonds…" (*Koran*, 47:4). And once the faithful Muslim has dispatched the infidel from this world, Allah is waiting to punish him forevermore in the next. "And those who disbelieve — for them awaits a draught of boiling water, and a painful chastisement for their disbelieving" (*Koran,* 10:4).

A few paragraphs back, I said that there isn't much a Muslim shouldn't do **to** a Kafir. Actually, there is something a Muslim should never do to a Kafir: make one his friend. "And whosoever takes them for friends, those — they are the evildoers" (*Koran*, 60:9). "Let not the believers take the unbelievers [Kafirs] for friends, rather than the believers — for whoso does that belongs not to God in anything — unless you have a fear of them" (*Koran*, 3:28). "O believers, take not My enemy and your enemy for friends, offering them love, though they have disbelieved in the truth that has come to you, expelling the Messenger and you because you believe in God your Lord. If you go forth to struggle in My way and seek My good pleasure, secretly loving them, yet I know very well what you conceal and what you publish; and whosoever of you does that, has gone astray from the right way" (*Koran*, 60:1). "Believers are friends one to the other to the exclusion of outsiders" (*Sira*, 342). In other words, it is ungodly to have a Kafir friend. Again from the *Sira*: "'O you who believe, do not choose those outside our community as intimate friends. They will spare no pains to corrupt you longing for your ruin'... you have more right to hate them than they to hate you" (*Sira*, 388). However, you may **act** like a Kafir is your friend if you are in a relatively weak position ("have fear of them" as quoted above in *Koran,* 3:28). Examples of situations where it would be permissible for a Muslim to act like a Kafir were his friend would include nations and cultures where Muslims are in a minority and in international relations where an Islamic nation is weaker than a negotiating partner. This pretense of friendship, however, is merely a feint until the Muslim or Muslim nation is in a stronger position to either convert, enslave, or kill the Kafir; and make no mistake about it, these are the only three options available for Karirs: conversion, enslavement, or death.

Every non-Muslim is a Kafir, but Muhammad and his followers have historically reserved a special enmity for two classes of Kafirs in particular: Jews and Christians. "O believers, take not Jews and Christians as friends; they are friends of each other. Whoso of you makes them his friends is one of them. God guides not the people of evildoers" (*Koran*, 5:51). Let's consider these two groups more closely.

Jews.

Muhammad had a bi-polar, love-hate relationship with the Jews — although it was the "south pole" and the "hate relationship" that ultimately won out. From the beginning of his ministry, Muhammad founded his claim to be a messenger of god upon Hebrew theology and Jewish customs. He began by asserting that he had received his revelations from Allah through the angel Gabriel. This was the same angel Gabriel who played key roles in both the Old and New Testaments. Muhammad professed the divine authority of the "Book;" namely, the *Torah* which had been delivered by God through Moses. He spoke glowingly about many of the heroes of the Old Testament and told many of the tales found therein — although with numerous, self-serving modifications. He also spoke well of Jesus and His Gospel message — again, with various self-serving nuances. Thus, Muhammad linked himself with a long line of Jewish prophets and presented himself as the last and greatest link in that chain. By doing all this, he wedded himself inextricably with the Jews and the Jewish tradition.

During the honeymoon phase of their relationship, Muhammad had many endearing things to say about the Jews. Muhammad passed on Allah's praise in these words from the *Koran*, "Indeed, We gave the Children of Israel the Book, the Judgment, and the Prophethood, and We provided them with good things, and We preferred them above all beings" (*Koran*, 45:16). "We gave to Moses [Musa] the Book and the Salvation..." (*Koran*, 2:53). "Children of Israel, remember My blessing wherewith I blessed you, and that I have preferred you above all beings..." (*Koran*, 2:40).

This marriage of convenience between Muhammad and the Jews enjoyed a warm and cordial honeymoon while Muhammad was still in Mecca — where there were virtually no Jews to contest his stories and his claim to prophethood. It was when he moved north to Medina that the marriage hit the skids and the Jews became detestable swine. Why? Because now there were Jews around — quite a few of them, in fact — who not only disputed his accounts of the Old Testament stories, but who had the audacity to refuse Muhammad's invitation to join him in an Islamic adulation of Allah — and, of course, Allah's greatest prophet.

The divine revelations Muhammad received about the Jews changed drastically once he moved to Medina. The Jews went from "preferred" by Allah to abhorred by him. The people once chosen to be God's light unto the world were now condemned to a dark fate. This, of course, gave Allah's messenger license to go on the attack. Consider the following.

"Then you turned away, all but a few of you, swerving aside" (*Koran*, 2:83). "But God has cursed them for their unbelief and only a few will believe" (*Sira*, 390) (*Koran*, 4:46). "Allah's Apostle said, 'May Allah curse the Jews, because Allah made fat illegal for them but they sold it and ate its price'" (Bukhari, 3:427). "Allah's Apostle said, "May Allah's curse be on the Jews for they built the places of worship at the graves of the Prophets" (Bukhari, 1:428). "Our attack upon God's enemy cast terror among the Jews, and there was no Jew in Medina who did not fear for his life" (*Sira*, 552). "The apostle said, 'Kill any Jew that falls into your power.' Thereupon Muhayyisa b. Mas'ud leapt upon Ibn Sunayna, a Jewish merchant with whom they had social and business relations, and killed him" (*Sira*, 554). "Allah's Apostle said, 'You (i.e. Muslims) will fight with the Jews till some of them will hide behind stones. The stones will (betray them) saying, "O Abdullah (i.e. slave of Allah)! There is a Jew hiding behind me; so kill him"'" (Bukhari, 4:176). "Once the Prophet went out after sunset and heard a dreadful voice, and said, "The Jews are being punished in their graves" (Bukhari, 2:457). Muhammad said, "A tribe of Jews disappeared. I do not know what became of them, but I think they changed and became rats. Have you noticed that a rat won't drink camel's milk, but it will drink goat's milk?" (Muslim, 042,7135). Elsewhere, Muhammad referred to Jews as apes (*Koran*, 2:65).

Muhammad's obsession with Jews and Christians alike even overshadowed his imminent death. "When the last moment of the life of Allah's Apostle came he started putting his 'Khamisa' [a square garment with markings on it] on his face and when he felt hot and short of breath he took it off his face and said, 'May Allah curse the Jews and Christians for they built the places of worship at the graves of their prophets" (Bukhari, 1:427).

The Jews have been instrumental to the evolution of Islam. The beheading of several hundred Jewish men and the enslavement of their women and children after the siege of Qurayza helped to establish the Islamic model of terror by which the Muslims would spread their regime across three continents. The practice of dhimmitude (to be discussed shortly) was initiated after the conquest of another Jewish community, Khaybar. Ever since the time of Muhammad, an unquenchable hatred of the Jews has helped to stoke the fires of Islamic aggression and savage terror around the world.

Christians.

As was the case with the Jews, Muhammad's relationship with the Christians had a decidedly bi-polar element as well, although it was not as rabid as his relationship with the Jews. A novice peruser of the *Koran* might conclude that Muhammad and Islam had a strong affinity with and affection for the Christians. As we have said, initially, Muhammad tried to establish his credentials by linking himself with the New Testament as well as the Old. The same angel Gabriel who told Mary that she would give birth to the Christ Child also — according to Muhammad — gave Allah's Prophet his revelations which he transcribed as the *Koran*. Muhammad acknowledged Jesus as great prophet and even referred to him as "Messiah" in the *Koran*. "And We gave to Moses the Book, and after him sent succeeding Messengers; and We gave Jesus [Isa] son of Mary [Marium] the clear signs, and confirmed him with the Holy Spirit…" (*Koran*, 2:87). And so, it might seem to a casual observer — or deliberate deceiver — that Islam and Christianity are fraternal twins. Hardly.

Remember that Muhammad claimed that both the Old Testament and the Gospel had been perverted to suit the interests of religious leaders and to remove any mention of the coming of Allah's greatest prophet; namely, himself. Among men, only Muhammad knew the true story of the Gospel because Gabriel had revealed it to him. According to Muhammad, the real "Good News" was not that God so loved the world that He gave his only Son so that whoever believed in him would receive eternal life. True, Jesus was a good guy — in fact, a really good guy — but He wasn't divine and He wasn't God's Son, and so there was no salvation to be received through believing in Him. There is no Trinity, there was no crucifixion, and so there was no resurrection. In effect, Muhammed condemned Jesus with false praise and then attempted to gut the whole salvation message of Christianity by denying Christ's divinity, death, and resurrection. Sounds like the kind of religion that a truly Evil One would concoct.

Islam offers a different kind of "good news" that just doesn't sound very good after one has heard the message of Christ. Paradise was not a gift to be received through faith in a beautiful act of divine grace and sacrifice. Paradise was earned by acknowledging Allah and his apostle and through the endless and tedious repetition of daily prayers, paying alms, making pilgrimages, fasting, and practicing a profusion of piddling minutia — oh yes, and killing as many Kafirs as you can in the process. Let us now look at some of the features of Christianity through the lens of Muhammad.

According to Muhammad, Jesus was a great prophet Who was sent by God. "When the angels said, 'Mary, God gives thee good tidings of a Word from Him whose name is Messiah, Jesus, son of Mary; high honored shall he be in this world and the next, near stationed to God. He shall speak to men in the cradle, and of age, and righteous he shall be.''Lord,' said Mary, 'how shall I have a son seeing no mortal has touched me?''Even so,' God said, 'God creates what He will'" (*Koran*, 3:45-47).

But, what Muhammad giveth, Muhammad taketh away. Muhammad acknowledged the preeminence of Jesus among men, but insisted that he was only a man and not divine, which completely undermines the main premise of Christianity. "Truly, the likeness of Jesus, in God's sight; is as Adam's likeness: He created him of dust then said unto him, 'Be', and he was" (*Koran*, 3:59). So much for the Christian tenet that Jesus was "begotten, not made."

Muhammad also contended that Christians are deluded when it comes to the real "good tidings" that Jesus taught. The most important point of Jesus' message was not about salvation through accepting Him as Savior, but rather about the coming of the last and greatest prophet, namely — you guessed it — Muhammad. "And when Jesus son of Mary said, 'Children of Israel, I am indeed the Messenger of God to you, confirming the Torah that is before me, and giving good tidings of a Messenger who shall come after me, whose name shall be Ahmad'" (*Koran*, 61:6). By the way, the name "Ahmad" means "highly praised" and has the same root as "Muhammad."

Muhammad was emphatic — and very repetitive — on the matter of Jesus' mortality. Jesus was not divine and certainly was not God's Son. "The Messiah, son of Mary, was only a Messenger; Messengers before him passed away..." (*Koran*, 5:75). "They are unbelievers who say, 'God is the Messiah, Mary's son'" (*Koran*, 5:17). "God has not taken to Himself any son..." (*Koran*, 23:91). "It is not for God to take a son unto Him" (*Koran*, 19:35). "And they say, 'The All-merciful has taken unto Himself a son.' You have indeed advanced something hideous!" (*Koran*, 19:91-92). "He has not taken to Him a son..." (*Koran*, 25:2).

"Praise belongs to God who has sent down upon His servant the Book [*Koran*]… to warn those who say, 'God has taken to Himself a son'; they have no knowledge of it, they nor their fathers; a monstrous word it is, issuing out of their mouths; they say nothing but a lie" (*Koran*, 18:4-5). Those who claim the divinity of Jesus are vile deceivers. As Muhammad said, "You lie. Your assertion that God has a son, your worship of the cross, and your eating pork hold you back from submission" (*Sira*, 403).

According to Muhammad's version of the New Testament, even Jesus denied His divinity and denounced the concept of the Trinity. "They are unbelievers who say, 'God is the Messiah, Mary's son.' For the Messiah said, 'Children of Israel, serve Allah, my Lord and your Lord. Verily whoso associates with God anything, God shall prohibit him entrance to Paradise, and his refuge shall be the Fire; and wrongdoers shall have no helpers.' They are unbelievers who say, 'God is the Third of Three.' No god is there but One God" (*Koran*, 5:72-73). "The Messiah, Jesus son of Mary, was only the Messenger of God, and His Word that He committed to Mary, and a Spirit from Him. So believe in God and His Messengers, and say not 'Three.' Refrain; better is it for you. God is only One God" (*Koran*, 4:171). Muhammed even took to calling Christians "polytheists" — believers in several gods — because of their belief in the Trinity: Father Son, and Holy Spirit.

What about the crucifixion and resurrection — two historically documented facts? Well, they simply did not happen, according to Muhammad. The *Koran* says, "yet they did not slay him, neither crucified him, only a likeness of that was shown to them. Those who are at variance concerning him surely are in doubt regarding him; they have no knowledge of him, except the following of surmise; and they slew him not of a certainty — no indeed; God raised him up to Him; God is All-mighty, All-wise" (*Koran*, 4:158-158).

So, then, what should be done about these Christian deceivers? If you have read this far, you should be able to guess the answer. Muhammad declared, "kill the polytheists wherever you find them, and seize them and besiege them and lie in wait for them in every ambush. But if they repent and perform prayer and pay the poor-tax, then let them go their way. God is forgiving, merciful" (*Sira*, 920). "On his return from Tabuk a messenger brought a letter from the kings of Himyar with their acceptance of Islam…" (*Sira*, 955). Included in this letter was an account of how the Islamic converts of Himyar had executed the polytheists. Muhammad's response included these words: "Your messenger… informed us of your Islam and of your killing the polytheists. God has guided you with His guidance" (*Sira*, 956). Muhammad also responded, "Malik b. Murra al-Rahawi has told me that you were the first of Himyar to accept Islam and have killed the polytheists, and I congratulate you…" (*Sira*, 957).

To summarize, according to Muhammad, Jesus was born of Mary by virgin birth. He was a great prophet, but a Muslim one. He was not divine. He was not the Son of God. He was not crucified and brought back to life but was taken up directly to Paradise. He will return in order to establish Sharia Law. Jesus was a Muslim, and "true Christians" are those who deny the Trinity and accept Muhammad as the final prophet. The New Testament, like the Old Testament, is corrupt and only the *Koran* contains the truth.

The Options for Kafirs.

The subtitle of this book is, "What You Need to Know About the World's Most Dangerous Religion." Although Islamic apologists and those who are ignorant about Muhammad and his religious creation will no doubt try to dismiss this claim as the rantings of a frothing "Islamophobe," surely by this time the reader has concluded from Islam itself that this is no gracious and tolerant religion that is content to coexist with nonbelievers. It is a profoundly bigoted and savage belief system that will not long permit opposition. In few places is this truth easier to see than in the options which Islam offers to those who have not yet submitted to its tenets. Listen to the "Verse of the Sword" taken from what is perhaps the last sura written by Muhammad. "Then, when the sacred months are drawn away, slay the idolaters wherever you find them, and take them, and confine them, and lie in wait for them at every place of ambush. But if they repent, and perform the prayer, and pay the alms, then let them go their way; God is All-forgiving, All-compassionate" (*Koran*, 9:5). As is often the case with Koranic verses, the meaning of this passage is obscured a bit by the flowery style of the writing. Here is the translation: "if they [Kafirs] repent, and perform the prayer, and pay the alms, then let them go their way…." Translation: Give non-believers a chance to convert. If they become Muslims, good. Leave them alone. But if they don't, then "lie in wait for them at every place of ambush" [hunt them down], "slay the idolaters" [kill them], or "confine them" [enslave them]. Conversion, death, or slavery.

These same choices were repeated elsewhere by Muhammad. "When you meet your enemies who are polytheists [anyone believing in more than one god, including Christians who, according to Muhammad, believe in three], invite them to three courses of action… Invite them to accept Islam; if they respond to you, accept it from them and desist from fighting against them… If they refuse to accept Islam, demand from them the Jizya [a poll tax for non-Muslims which was associated with a system of slavery called "dhimmitude" to be discussed shortly]. If they agree to pay, accept it from them and hold of your hands. If they refuse to pay the tax, seek Allah's help and fight them" (Muslim, 19:4294).

The Islamic outreach plan to nonbelievers consists of a simple, three-part program. (1) Offer Kafirs the opportunity to convert. If they do, and begin to live a good, Muslim life, leave them alone. If they do not convert, then either (2) enslave them (classic slavery, prison, or dhimmitude), or (3) kill them. "Coexist" is not an option — unless the Muslim finds himself in a weak position relative to the Kafir, in which case, he appeases and deceives him (remember, "Jihad is deceit") until he is in a position of strength and can offer the Kafir the primary three options.

Option Two, slavery, has been a very successful Islamic tool for suppressing and exhausting the opposition, while making some money along the way. It has been so instrumental to the history of Islam and to the peoples it has encountered, that we really need to consider it in more detail.

CHAPTER TWELVE

SLAVERY AND DHIMMITUDE

For the most part, slavery is a positive thing within Islam. With the sole exception of prohibiting Muslims from enslaving fellow Muslims, you will be hard-pressed to find the word "slavery" used in a negative way throughout the *Koran*, *Sira*, or Hadith. Recall that a good Muslim sees himself as a slave of Allah, and that is exactly how Allah sees humankind — as his slaves.

Remember that Muhammad is the exemplar — the ideal Muslim — and he was involved in virtually every aspect of slavery. Ransoming prisoners and selling slaves were among the first profit centers of Islam and were used by Muhammad to finance his jihad. Muhammad owned several slaves — including black slaves — and was a slave-trader. He enslaved the women and children of many of the settlements he conquered. He kept sex slaves for his own pleasure. In fact, one of his favorite sex partners was a beautiful Coptic slave named Mariyah who bore him a son named Ibrahim. He gave slaves as gifts and passed around slaves for the sexual gratification of his closest associates, known as "Companions." Muhammad also approved of slave-owners raping their female slaves.

It is true that a Muslim receives a great deal of credit for manumitting, or emancipating, a slave; but they don't free Kafirs. A Kafir slave must first convert to Islam before being eligible for emancipation. Even then it is not required. Still, the prospect of freedom provides a great incentive for converting.

Given Muhammad's proclivities and his official blessing of slavery, it should come as no surprise that Islam has been instrumental in the institution of slavery for nearly a millennium and one-half. Islam also played a critical role in the slave trade that sent most of the African slaves to America. We have a perception — conjured by politically correct textbooks and Hollywood movies — of unscrupulous white merchants sailing off the west coast of Africa where they disembarked and raided local tribes and villages, kidnapping innocent natives, chaining them up, and transporting them brutally across the Atlantic to seaports in America where they were sold at slave markets. Actually, most of that is generally true. The portion that is not true is the part about raiding "local tribes and villages, kidnapping innocent natives." They didn't have to go to the trouble. Muslims had already taken care of that part of the business for them.

Muslims ran slave markets along the west coast of Africa much like someone would set up a produce stand. They gathered Africans who would not submit to Islam, chained them up in market places, and sold them like chickens or pigs to the merchants who came shopping. It has been estimated that about twenty-five million Africans have been sold as slaves by Muslim slave-traders. Roughly eleven million of them were sold in the Americas. Tragically, the grisly business continues to this day. It truly is ironic that African-Americans constitute the most fertile ground for Islamic recruitment in America. It was the Muslims who wrote a very long and dreadful chapter in their history — the history of slavery. By the way, Muslim slave-traders seemed to hold a bias that should outrage the African-Americans who find Islam so attractive today. The highest priced slaves in Mecca were white women. The price of a female white slave ran from three to ten times the rate of black women. Black lives may matter to Muslim slave-traders, but not as much as White lives.

The economic incentive for slavery to Muslims has been consistent and powerful. But there has been another motivation for — and application of — slavery that has fit neatly into the Islamic master plan for global domination: recruitment. This is where "dhimmitude" enters the scene.

In 629 Muhammad's Muslim army attacked the Jewish settlement of Khaybar, an oasis community about 93 miles from Medina. The Muslims already had a well-established reputation for brutality — especially among Jews. So, when defeat seemed imminent, the Jews of

Khaybar suggested terms of surrender that were simply irresistible to Muhammad the merchant. If Muhammad would allow the Jews to live and stay on their land, they would surrender one-half of their produce to him every year. The return on investment was simply too tempting to pass up. Muhammad agreed, and the institution of dhimmitude was born. Let's look at the documentation.

"The Prophet made a deal with the people of Khaibar [also spelled "Khaybar"] that they would have half the fruits and vegetation of the land they cultivated"(Bukhari, 3:522). "Allah's Apostle gave the land of Khaibar to the Jews on the condition that they work on it and cultivate it, and be given half of its yield" (Bukhari, 3:524).

The Arabic word "Dhimmis" means both "protected" and "guilty." Under this agreement, Jews and Christians are considered "protected" because there is a loose contractual agreement which allows them to live in Islamic states, but not as equals with the Muslims. Jews and Christians are considered "guilty" because they have not submitted to Allah and his true prophet, Muhammad.

The most salient condition of dhimmitude is that the dhimmi must pay a tax known as "jizya," which can be up to fifty percent of all his wealth and annual earnings. But that's not all. A great many other restrictions and humiliations have been imposed on the dhimmis over the centuries, which were designed to impoverish them and wear down their resistance to converting to Islam. For example, in addition to paying the jizya, it was often ordered that the tax be collected in a humiliating way, like striking the dhimmi on the head or back of the neck or holding his beard and striking both cheeks. Dhimmis often were not allowed to dress like Muslims or seek to resemble them. They had to wear their customary clothing or other special clothing, indicating that they were dhimmis. Muslims wanted to make sure the dhimmi was recognized so he could be treated like the low-life Kafir scum that he was. Similarly, dhimmis were occasionally required to cut the front of their hair, which is an Arabic sign of shame and humiliation. Dhimmis could not show any religious symbols outside their homes and churches. They often were permitted to ride a donkey, but not a horse. They could not use saddles. They could not carry any kind of weapon. They had to keep to the side of the street and out of the way of Muslims. If riding on a public conveyance, they had to move if a Muslim wanted his seat. Dhimmis may not proselytize among Muslims nor testify against them, although Muslims may testify against dhimmis. They may not build any structure that is higher than a Muslim building. The list goes on, and if a dhimmi should violate these terms, he may be sold into full-fledged slavery or killed.

The terms of this "contract" can always be modified or revoked by the Muslims, as the Jews of Khaybar discovered. After being defeated, they were allowed to stay on their land for several more years, but were ultimately expelled by Caliph Umar. "Umar [the second successor or Caliph after Muhammad] expelled the Jews and the Christians from Hijaz [also "Hejaz" — the district where

Khaybar is located]. When Allah's Apostle had conquered Khaibar, he wanted to expel the Jews from it as its land became the property of Allah, His Apostle, and the Muslims. Allah's Apostle intended to expel the Jews but they requested him to let them stay there on the condition that they would do the labor and get half of the fruits. Allah's Apostle told them, 'We will let you stay on this condition, as long as we wish.' So, they (i.e. Jews) kept on living there until Umar forced them to go towards Taima and Ariha" (Bukhari, 3:531).

Dhimmitude is a state of virtual slavery. Its purpose is two-fold: (1) to fill Islamic coffers with the jizya tax imposed on the dhimmi and (2) to grind down the resistance of non-believers within the society until they finally submitted and accepted Islam. The economic motivation for dhimmitude is clear in this passage: "We said to Umar bin Al-Khattab, 'O Chief of the believers! Advise us.' He said, 'I advise you to fulfill Allah's Convention (made with the Dhimmis) as it is the convention of your Prophet and the source of the livelihood of your dependents (i.e. the taxes from the Dhimmis)'" (Bukhari, 4:388). Dhimmitude's power as a "recruiting" tool is evident wherever Islamic rule is established. Historically, nearly all the non-Islamic population of a nation disappeared within two or three generations of the onset of an Islamic administration.

The advance of Islam has been financed with the plunder of ill-gotten gains. Without the loot derived from outright theft, the slave trade, and the taxes paid by the dhimmi, the Islamic community in the world would be poor and unable to sustain itself. Islamic apologists often point to the cultural and scientific advances provided by Islamic culture, but a little closer look reveals that virtually all of the alleged advances (including so-called "Arabic" numerals and the invention of the Zero — which actually was developed by Hindus) were in fact stolen, not spawned, by Islam. The same can be said about Islamic wealth. Without plunder and oil, the Islamic world would be a destitute, poverty-stricken hovel.

CHAPTER THIRTEEN

ALLAH IS NOT ABBA

The Allah depicted by his messenger, Muhammad, is a harsh taskmaster, to say the least. He insists upon a slavish compliance with ritual. He is intolerant of insubordination and commands the enslavement and genocide of those who do not submit to his will. Modern-day Jews and Christians alike are often repulsed by such an appalling and vicious depiction of god. It is easy to see why the Christians and Jews who are familiar with Allah would feel this way. But what can we say to the Muslims who are familiar with Jehovah and who make the same claim about Him? The Bible certainly makes it easy to lodge a similar complaint. Let's take a look.

"Then the Lord rained upon Sodom and upon Gomorrah brimstone and fire from the Lord out of heaven; and He overthrew those cities, and all the plain, and all the inhabitants of the cities, and that which grew upon the ground" (Genesis 19:24-25).

147

"And they warred against the Midianites, as the Lord commanded Moses; and they slew all the males" (Numbers 31:7). "And Moses said unto them, 'Have ye saved all the women alive?'... 'Now therefore kill every male among the little ones, and kill every woman that hath known man by lying with him. But all the women children, that have not known a man by lying with him, keep alive for yourselves'" (Numbers 31:15, 17-18).

"When the Lord thy God shall bring thee into the land whither thou goest to possess it, and hath cast out many nations before thee, the Hittites, and the Girgashites, and the Amorites, and the Canaanites, and the Perizzites, and the Hivites, and the Jebusites, seven nations greater and mightier than thou; and when the Lord thy God shall deliver them before thee; thou shalt smite them, and utterly destroy them; thou shalt make no covenant with them, nor shew mercy unto them..." (Deuteronomy 7:1-2).

"When thou comest nigh unto a city to fight against it, then proclaim peace unto it. And it shall be, if it make thee answer of peace, and open unto thee, then it shall be, that all the people that is found therein shall be tributes unto thee, and they shall serve thee. And if it will make no peace with thee, but will make war against thee, then thou shalt besiege it: and when the Lord thy God hath delivered it into thine hands, thou shalt smite every male thereof with the edge of the sword; but the women, and the little ones, and the cattle, and all that is in the city, even all the spoil thereof, thou shalt eat the spoil of thine enemies, which the Lord thy God hath given thee. Thus shalt thou do unto all the cities which are very far off from thee, which are not of the cities of these nations. But of the cities of these people, which the Lord thy God doth give thee for an inheritance, thou shalt save alive nothing that breathest: but thou shalt utterly destroy them; namely the Hittites, and the Amonites, the Canaanites, and the Perizzites, the Hivites, and the Jebusites; as the Lord thy God hath commanded thee…" (Deuteronomy 20:10-17).

"Thus saith the Lord of hosts, 'I remember that which Amalek did to Israel, how he laid wait for him in the way, when he came up from Egypt. Now go and smite Amalek, and utterly destroy all that they have and spare them not; but slay both man and woman, infant and suckling, ox and sheep, camel and ass'" (1 Samuel 15:2-3).

"And they entered into a covenant to seek the Lord God of their fathers with all their heart and with all their soul; that whosoever would not seek the Lord God of Israel should be put to death, whether small or great, whether man or woman" (2 Chronicles 15:12-13).

These chilling Biblical commands to kill, enslave, and take plunder sound positively Islamic. It would be easy for a superficial observer to paint Jehovah and Allah with the same brush and dismiss them both as anachronistic manifestations of a more savage and superstitious time. But, as they say, the Devil is in the details. Well, in this case, so is God; and a more detailed comparison between Jehovah and Allah will reveal some important distinctions. I will point out just two.

Whereas Allah's condemnation of non-Muslims is universal and eternal, Jehovah's condemnation of non-Jews was specific and short-term. The targets of Jehovah's wrath were generally vicious peoples who practiced savage barbarity (gee, who does that sound like?) and who stood in the way of establishing a righteous, Israelite homeland (gee, who does that sound like?). So, whereas Jehovah was a sniper who accurately targeted very specific prey which were narrowly defined by time and space, Allah drops nukes on all non-Muslims everywhere for all time. Jehovah can be likened to a loving and strong parent who, reluctantly and regrettably, must occasionally discipline his errant children. Allah is more like the abusive slave-master (Muhammad's own description of Allah) who not only delights in punishing his errant slaves, but who seeks out the opportunity to do so.

The real distinction between Allah and Jehovah, however, only becomes apparent when we introduce the "Abba Attribute" of Jehovah — which is exactly what Jesus did. For those unfamiliar with the word "abba," it is the Aramaic word for "father." Aramaic is the language which Jesus spoke, and the word He often used when referring to God was "Abba." There is an interesting and revealing linguistic detail, however, which must not be overlooked, or the true impact of the word "abba" — and of our relationship with Him — will be lost. Linguists will tell us that, although the word "abba" does refer to the male parent, the word itself is actually the diminutive form of the word for "father." And so, though it is rarely translated this way, apparently for fear of seeming disrespectful, "abba" really means "daddy" or "papa." Think about what that says about our relationship with God. To help you plumb the depths of this subject, think about the differences between the words "father," "dad," and "daddy." "Father" is respectful but formal, cold, and distant. "Dad" is more warm, affectionate, and friendly. But "Daddy" is a term which expresses the deepest intimacy, the purest adoration, and the greatest trust. Jesus knew that in God, we have a daddy. Abba.

Although Muhammad often referred to Allah as "merciful" and "compassionate," it's a hard case to make. It is unlikely that either Muhammad or any of his Muslims have ever called Allah, "Daddy." Allah sees his believers as "slaves" and the non-believers as expendable trash. "God loveth not the unbelievers" (*Sira*, 406). Abba, on the other hand, sees all humans as his children — whether they believe or not. Allah waits for sinners to come to him before blessing them. Abba seeks His children so they can be reconciled to Him. He is the Good Shepherd who goes looking for His lost sheep. "But God demonstrates His own love for us in this; while we were still sinners, Christ died for us… when we were God's enemies, we were reconciled to Him through the death of His Son…'" (Romans 5:8,10). Allah keeps a fastidious account of our good deeds and bad deeds and weighs them precisely to see who deserves Paradise and who deserves Hell. Abba offers salvation and Heaven as a free gift to His beloved children if only they have faith and accept His Son, Jesus, as Savior. "For by grace you have been saved, through faith — and this not from yourselves, it is the gift of God — not by works, so that no one can boast" (Ephesians 2:8-9).

Well, we can quote verses and argue theology all we want, but for me, the greatest demonstration of the difference between Allah and Abba was shown in the face of a former Muslim woman whom I met some years ago. She had immigrated from Iran to the United States a few years earlier and had become a Christian. Her eyes shone, her face glowed, and her voice overflowed with joy as she talked about her relationship with Jesus and her Abba. A thought popped to mind, and I asked her, "Tell me, did you ever feel this way about Allah?" The light of joy that had beamed from her visage was instantly extinguished at the thought of her old master. An eerie look of dread — quite like someone recalling a horrifying nightmare— filled her eyes. "Oh, no," she said quietly, while shaking her head slightly. "We were afraid of Allah."

It also is commonplace for deceivers and the ignorant to favorably compare Muhammad and Jesus. Certainly, Muhammad did as much. "I heard Allah's Apostle saying, 'I am the nearest of all the people to the son of Mary, and all the prophets are paternal brothers, and there has been no prophet between me and him (i.e. Jesus)'" (Bukhari, 4:651). Again, "Allah's Apostle said, 'Both in this world and in the Hereafter, I am the nearest of all the people to Jesus, the son of Mary. The prophets are paternal brothers, their mothers are different, but their religion is one" (Bukhari, 4:652). Still, Muhammad warns, "Do not exaggerate in praising me as the Christians praised the son of Mary, for I am only a Slave. So, call me the Slave of Allah and His Apostle" (Bukhari, 4:654). Muhammad did not claim to be divine, and he attributed the same mortality to Jesus.

Elsewhere, Muhammad made it clear that his feelings about Jesus were not merely his own conjectures but were the result of divine revelations. According to Muhammad, Allah explained to him that "... though I gave Jesus power over those matters in virtue of which they say that he is God such as raising the dead, healing the sick, creating birds of clay, and declaring the unseen, I made him thereby a sign to men and a confirmation of his prophethood wherewith I sent him to his people. But some of my majesty and power I withheld from him such as appointing kings by a prophetic command and placing them where I wished, and making the night to pass into day and the day into night and bringing forth the living from the dead and the dead from the living and nurturing whom I will without stint, both the good and the evil man. All that I withheld from Jesus and gave him no power over it. Have they not an example and a clear proof that if he were a god that all would be within his power, while they know that he fled from kings and because of them he moved about the country from town to town" (*Sira*, 406). Yes, Jesus was a great moral teacher and prophet, but not the divine Son of God; and Muhammad was instructed "to warn those who say God has taken a son" (*Sira*, 193).

The similarities that Muhammad claimed between himself and Jesus were the product of his self-serving conception of Jesus. Muhammad's Jesus is not the Jesus Whom Christians know. According to Muhammad, Jesus was a Muslim Who served Allah, not Abba. Muhammad asserted that "By Him in Whose Hands my soul is, surely (Jesus,) the son of Mary will soon descend amongst you and will judge mankind justly (as a Just Ruler)..." (Bukhari, 4:657). Undoubtedly, that sounds familiar to Christians, but then Muhammad went on to add, "How will you be when the son of Mary (i.e. Jesus) descends amongst you and he will judge people by the Law of the Quran and not by the law of Gospel?" (Bukhari, 4:658). Oops, it seems that the second coming of Jesus will find Him imposing Sharia Law and not consummating the love of the Father. Another passage finds Jesus enforcing a very temporal and materialistic type of administration upon His return. "Allah's Apostle said, 'By Him in Whose Hands my soul is, son of Mary (Jesus) will shortly descend amongst you people (Muslims) as a just ruler and will break the Cross and kill the pig and abolish the Jizya (a tax taken from the non-Muslims, who are in the protection, of the Muslim government). Then there will be abundance of money and no-body will accept charitable gifts" (Bukhari, 3:425 & 3:656). Not exactly straight out of *Revelation*.

A brief comparison of the words and deeds of Muhammad and Jesus will quickly reveal them to be as different as night and day — or evil and good.

Muhammad despised those who did not accept him and his religion. "O believers, take not My enemy and your enemy for friends, offering them love, though they have disbelieved in the truth that has come to you, expelling the Messenger and you because you believe in God your Lord. If you go forth to struggle in My way and seek My good pleasure, secretly loving them, yet I know very well what you conceal and what you publish; and whosoever of you does that, has gone astray from the right way" (*Koran*, 60:1). "And whosoever takes them for friends, those — they are the evildoers" (*Koran*, 60:9).

By comparison, Jesus loved even those who did not accept him and his religion. "But I say unto you, love your enemies, bless them that curse you, do good to them that hate you, and pray for them which despitefully use you, and persecute you…" (Matthew 5:44).

Muhammad repeatedly sought vengeance against those who offended him, and he taught his followers to do likewise. "Allah's Apostle sent a group of Ansari men to kill Abu-Rafi" (Bukhari, 4:264). Abu al-Rafi was one of the leaders of the Jewish tribes settled around the Khaybar oasis discussed earlier. He had attempted to raise an army to ward off the Muslim invaders, thereby incurring the wrath of Muhammad. "Abdullah bin Atik entered his house at night and killed him while he was sleeping" (Bukhari, 4:265). Abu al-Rafi's two brothers were also assassinated at Muhammad's orders. On another occasion, "Some people from Uraina tribe came to Medina and its climate did not suit them, so Allah's Apostle (p.b.u.h.)

["peace be unto him" or "praise be unto him"] allowed them to go to the herd of camels (given as Zakat) and they drank their milk and urine (as medicine) but they killed the shepherd and drove away all the camels. So Allah's Apostle sent (men) in their pursuit to catch them, and they were brought, and he had their hands and feet cut [off], and their eyes were branded with heated pieces of iron and they were left in the Harra (a stony place at Medina) biting the stones" (Bukhari, 2:577). The reference to "biting the stones" had to do with their reaction to profound thirst. Another Hadith tells the same story, but concludes, "They asked for water, and nobody provided them with water till they died…."

Jesus, on the other hand, forgave those who offended Him, and He taught His followers to do likewise. "And unto him that smiteth thee on the one cheek offer also the other; and him that taketh away thy cloak forbid not to take thy coat also" (Luke 6:29).

Muhammad permitted the use of lies to accomplish his goals. "The Prophet said, 'Who is ready to kill Ka'b bin Ashraf who has really hurt Allah and His Apostle?" (Bukhari, 4:270). Another Hadith points out that Ka'b bin Ashraf was "a Jew" and continued, "Muhammad bin Maslama replied, 'Do you like me to kill him?' The Prophet replied in the affirmative. Muhammad bin Maslama said, 'Then allow me to say what I like.' The Prophet replied, 'I do (i.e. allow you)'" (Bukhari 4:271). Other Hadiths make it clear that the request to "allow me to say what I like" was asking permission to lie. In fact, it was Maslama's deceitful words that enabled him to gain the confidence of K'ab bin Ashraf so he could get close enough to kill him.

Jesus, on the other hand, commended the truth. "But he that doeth truth cometh to the light, that his deeds may be made manifest, that they are wrought in God" (John 3:21). "Jesus saith unto him, 'I am the way, the truth, and the life: no man cometh unto the Father, but by me'" (John 14:6).

When Muhammad's opponents stealthfully approached him to glean information, Muhammad ordered them to be killed. "'An infidel spy came to the Prophet while he was on a journey. The spy sat with the companions of the Prophet and started talking and then went away. The Prophet said (to his companions), "Chase and kill him." So, I killed him.' The Prophet then gave him the belongings of the killed spy (in addition to his share of the war booty)" (Bukhari, 4:286).

When Jesus' opponents stealthfully approached Him to glean information, Jesus taught them. "And, behold, a certain lawyer stood up, and tempted him, saying, 'Master, what shall I do to inherit eternal life?' He said unto him, 'What is written in the law?' How readest thou?' And he answering said, 'Thou shalt love the Lord thy God with all thy heart, and with all thy soul, and with all thy strength, and with all thy mind; and thy neighbor as thyself.' And He said unto him, 'Thou hast answered right: this do, and thou shalt live.' But he, willing to justify himself, said unto Jesus, 'And who is my neighbor?'" (Luke 10:25-29). At that point Jesus told the parable of the Good Samaritan.

Muhammad was a strict legalist who showed no mercy to those who violated the law — unless, as we have seen, it was himself. "The Jew brought to the Prophet a man and a woman from amongst them who have committed (adultery) illegal sexual intercourse. He ordered both of them to be stoned (to death), near the place of offering the funeral prayers beside the mosque" (Bukhari, 2:413). And again, "The Prophet said, 'O Unais! Go to the wife of this (man) and if she confesses (that she has committed illegal sexual intercourse), then stone her to death" (Bukhari, 3:508).

Jesus, however, understood that the law was all about God's love and should be administered accordingly. "And the scribes and Pharisees brought unto Him a woman taken in adultery; and when they had set her in the midst, they say unto him, 'Master, this woman was taken in adultery, in the very act. Now Moses in the law commanded us, that such should be stoned: but what sayest thou?'... So when they continued asking Him, He lifted up Himself, and said unto them, 'He that is without sin among you, let him first cast a stone at her... And they which heard it, being convicted by their own conscience, went out one by one, beginning at the eldest, even unto the last: and Jesus was left alone, and the woman standing in the midst. When Jesus had lifted up himself, and saw none but the woman, He said unto her, 'Woman, where are those thine accusers? Hath no man condemned thee?' She said, 'No man, Lord.' And Jesus said unto her, 'Neither do I condemn thee: go, and sin no more'" (John 8: 3-11).

Muhammad captured free men and held them for ransom or killed them. Jesus freed guilty sinners by paying their ransom and then gave them eternal life.

Muhammad cursed those who cursed him. "Now Ubayy… when he used to meet the apostle in Mecca, would say, 'Muhammad, I have got a horse called Aud which I feed every day on many measures of corn. I shall kill you when I am riding it.' The apostle answered, 'No, I shall kill you, if God wills'" (*Sira*, 575).

Jesus pleaded for forgiveness for those who cursed, condemned, and crucified Him. "Father, forgive them; for they know not what they do" (Luke 23:34).

After being injured in the Battle of Uhud, Muhammad exclaimed, "The wrath of God is fierce against him who bloodied the face of His prophet" (*Sira*, 576). Whereas Muhammad called down Allah's wrath upon those who bloodied his prophet, Abba showered His love, grace, mercy, and forgiveness upon those who bloodied His Son.

During the roughly three years of his ministry, Jesus won acclaim among a diverse multitude, often speaking to thousands who came from far and wide to hear him. During the roughly thirteen years of his ministry in Mecca, Muhammad won the allegiance of only a few hundred followers. His attraction to the masses did not come about until after he had retooled himself into a vicious warlord, and he could pay people — or scare them — to follow him.

Muhammad formed an army to fight his enemies. Jesus did not. Muhammad attacked caravans and settlements, stealing and enslaving and killing. Jesus did not.

Muhammad taught and practiced violence and vengeance. Jesus did not. Muhammad ordered those who offended him to be tortured and killed. Jesus did not. Muhammad lived to enslave and kill those whom he believed to be the adversaries of God. Jesus died to free and save those who were the adversaries of God.

To argue "Jehovah" and "Allah" are basically two different names for the same deity — and to maintain that Jesus and Muhammad are essentially similar — are either expressions of unconscionable ignorance or the vilest evil.

CHAPTER FOURTEEN

HISTORY

From the early days in Medina, violent aggression has been the mainstay of Muslim foreign policy. Islam did not expand because it had an appealing theology. It expanded because it had a ruthless army that was willing to commit any type of atrocity in order to further its ends. The first victims were the various communities within the territory of modern-day Saudi Arabia; but even before Muhammad's death in 632, Islamic expansion had reached beyond the Arabic Peninsula.

Muhammad's closest Companion, Abu Bakr, (the same man who gave Muhammad his six-year-old daughter, Aisha, as a gift) was selected to be the caliph following the Apostle's death. The Shiites dispute this, but the historic record is fairly clear. A "caliph" is a generalissimo, king, and pope all rolled into one supreme and powerful package. He holds ultimate temporal and spiritual authority. Accordingly, the responsibility to continue the expansion of Islam fell directly upon

Abu Bakr's shoulders; but before he could commit completely to this task, he had another embarrassing distraction to handle. Once Muhammad was dead, throngs of Muslims wanted to leave the fold. It was, in effect, a slave revolt against the slave master, Allah. Abu Bakr responded in a manner that would have made his old, dead friend beam with pride. He executed the deserters and effectively convinced the other would-be apostates to remain faithful — whether they liked it or not. It was a practice that would continue to the present day.

Umar, another Companion of Muhammad, succeeded Abu Bakr as caliph and spent the next ten years committed to jihad against Egypt, Syria, Iraq, and Persia. Umar was killed by a Persian whom he had enslaved. Uthman was the next caliph. He ruled for twelve years and was killed by a grandson of Abu Bakr over a political dispute. His body was deposited on the town dump. Ali, another Companion of Muhammad, became the fourth caliph (first caliph if you have Shia leanings). He was implicated in the assassination of Uthman and was killed after a civil war of sorts broke out against Ali. That rebellion was led by Aisha, Abu Bakr's daughter and Muhammad's favorite wife. It appears that the sword has always been the main way for resolving disputes by Muslims — whether the dispute was with Kafirs or with each other.

By the end of his life, Muhammad had already unified much of the Arabian Peninsula under Islamic control. Mere Arabia, however, was too small of a target for Allah's messenger. Shortly before his death, "Allah's Apostle wrote to Caesar [ruler of the Byzantines] and invited him to Islam…" (Bukhari 4:191). In that letter, Muhammad wrote, "In the name of Allah, the most Beneficent, the most Merciful (This letter is) from Muhammad, the slave of Allah, and His Apostle, to Heraculius, the Ruler of the Byzantine. Peace be upon the followers of guidance. Now then, I invite you to Islam (i.e. surrender to Allah), embrace Islam and you will be safe; embrace Islam and Allah will bestow on you a double reward. But if you reject this invitation of Islam, you shall be responsible for misguiding the peasants (i.e. your nation)" (Bukhari, 4:191). Very shortly after Muhammad's death the Islamic invasion of the Byzantine Empire began.

The area of Gaza was sacked in 634. Damascus fell in 635, just three years after Muhammad's death. Al-Basrah, in Iraq, fell the next year. The savage siege against the Kafir world was just beginning, and now it has continued for nearly fourteen centuries.

Caliph Umar, the religious-political-military leader of Islam from 634-644, issued this order to his lieutenant Utbah ibn Ghazwan: "Summon the people to God; those who respond to your call, accept it from them, but those who refuse must pay the poll tax out of humiliation and lowliness. If they refuse this, it is the sword without leniency. Fear God with regard to what you have been entrusted" (*The History of al-Tabari, Vol 12*). In this order Umar perfectly followed the three-part instruction of Muhammad: offer the opportunity to convert, then enslave or kill those who do not accept.

By 638, both Antioch and Jerusalem had been taken. Keep in mind that Damascus, Antioch, Jerusalem, and much of the surrounding areas were largely Christian by this time. Islam had begun its quest for global domination, and its "evangelists" were not compassionate missionaries trying to enlighten the world; but rather, armies of jihadists seeking to enslave it.

In November of 642, Alexandria fell. Nearly all of Egypt had succumbed to the armies of Islam. The relentless advance continued. Huge swaths of land in the Middle East, north Africa, the Mediterranean, and south Europe were seized in a blatant and bloody orgy of aggression — and it would still be roughly four centuries before the first Crusade responded. (The First Crusade was commissioned by Pope Urban II in 1095.) In 712, Spain was invaded, and by 715, Muslim armies were on the verge of taking all of that nation, a trophy they held for over seven hundred years. It would not be until 1492 that the Spaniards would expel the Muslim hoards from their land. The assault pressed northward into France in 722. In 846, Islamic forces reached Rome and bullied a promise of tribute from the Pope.

Meanwhile, the east was not spared. An advance into present-day Afghanistan, Pakistan, and India began in the Eighth Century, and always the pattern was the same. Muslims viciously invaded countries whose only offense was that they were not Islamic. Those who did not convert were killed or enslaved.

After more than four centuries of Islamic aggression that forcefully seized about two-thirds of all the Christian lands, the followers of Jesus finally decided to stop turning the other cheek and instead committed to "destroy the works of the Devil" (1 John 3:8). The call for the First Crusade was issued by Pope Urban II in 1095. There were seven Crusades from 1098 to 1250. They were often savagely fought, and atrocities were committed on both sides. It must be emphasized, however, that the Crusades were defensive and not early examples of European imperialism. They all sought merely to reclaim what had been taken by Muslim aggression; and whereas the attacks of the Crusader numbered in the scores over about one-and-a-half centuries, Muslim assaults soared to several hundreds over many centuries.

Most of the accomplishments of the Crusaders were subsequently lost, but the Crusades did succeed in pushing back the Islamic lines and slowing their sweep across three continents. However, the relentless surge would begin anew, and more territory fell to the Muslim armies over the following centuries. Greece, Bulgaria, Serbia, Macedonia, Albania, Croatia all fell. And then Constantinople was seized by Muhammad's marauders. Islam spread like a malignancy across three continents and often decimated nearly all traces of the preceding cultures. By the way, the significance of "911" has nothing to do with the digits used to signify an emergency. After ages of aggression, the Islamic tide was finally stemmed by the Polish King John III Sobieski who thwarted the Muslims during their second assault on Vienna. It marked the high tide of Islamic expansion in Europe and the beginning of their retreat. The date of the battle was September 11,1683; and ever since "911" has symbolized the vow of vengeance for the defeat at Vienna.

The history of Islam is not only written in oceans of blood, its narrative is accompanied by the sorrowful and wretched clanking of chains. Islam, true to the model of Muhammad, has been one of the greatest practitioners of the slave trade in history — a history which they continue to write. Approximately twenty-five million slaves have been sold from Africa alone. As was mentioned earlier, but deserves repeating, it is especially ironic that we have an organization called the Black Muslims in the United States, and to read that the African-American population presents some of the most fertile ground for Islamic recruitment in America. The reason that most African-Americans are here in the United States is because they were captured by Muslims and then sold in Muslim slave markets to the merchants who brought them to North America. Despite the specious impressions conjured by Hollywood extravaganzas, politically correct and factually incorrect textbooks, and self-serving politicians, unscrupulous white men did not sail their ships to the west coast of Africa and then disembark teams of raiders to capture innocent natives peacefully living their lives. No, they pulled up to well-organized slave markets where the Muslims had already done the work of capturing and holding the natives for them. It's one of those dirty little secrets that many unprincipled people have an interest in keeping well-hidden.

From the minarets of Mecca and Tehran to — not so long ago — the podium of the president himself, there are those who try to dismiss the viciousness of Islam by comparing it to a similar nastiness within Christianity. Unfortunately for the deceivers, it is a "no sale" for those who know the truth. Following the death of Jesus, Christianity was outlawed and persecuted during the first three centuries of its existence. It struggled to survive. Following the death of Muhammad, Muslims faced no real organized nor sustained persecution. It fought to enslave and kill. And whereas the Christian church initially sent out missionaries to persuade non-believers about the truth of their faith, the Muslim leaders sent out marauding armies to convert, enslave, or murder non-believers. To be sure, Christianity has had its shameful episodes, but these were "episodes" and were perpetrated by men who violated the principles of their religion. On the other hand, the history of Islam is an almost unrelenting account of terror perpetrated my men who were following the principles of their religion.

History shows quite conclusively that all cultural and political systems that border Islamic nations or which include a significant number of Muslims ultimately fall to Islam or are mortally threatened by it. It is an aggressive, expansive, predatory, system. If we do not want to follow this pattern and become the next victims of Islam, then we must consider some tough realities and make some tough choices.

PART FOUR

RESPONDING TO THE THREAT

CHAPTER FIFTEEN

THE MYTH OF THE "MODERATE MUSLIM"

Islam has been described here as a "gang with a god" and as "an aggressive, expansive, predatory, system" that has waged a world war against non-believers for nearly fourteen centuries. It is not going to stop — not of its own accord, at least. The only three options it offers us Kafirs is conversion, enslavement, or death. But what if we don't want to convert, be enslaved, or die? Is there another option? Of course, but as we have seen, that option is not to coexist. Coexistence with Islam is a myth cherished by the deluded and a lie promulgated by the agents of Islam. The hard and unpleasant truth is this: as long as Islam exists, the existence of non-Muslims will always be in extreme jeopardy. The options for the non-Islamic world, therefore, are very similar to those of a cancer patient. He must either beat the disease into permanent remission, or destroy all the malignancy. If he fails to accomplish this, he dies.

But, really, that seems so harsh. Can't we all just get along? Can't we devise a strategy that would focus on strengthening the moderate Muslims while weakening the radicals?

What radicals? ISIS/ISIL, Hamas, Hezbollah, the Islamic Brotherhood, Al Queda, Taliban, Boko Haram? Those aren't radicals. That's mainstream Islam, as we have clearly seen from the documents of Islam itself.

What moderates? You mean the throngs that took to the streets to protest the kidnappings and bombings and beheadings and immolations and crucifixions and 911? Oh, that's right. We didn't see any of that, did we? Why do you suppose that is? To build a strategy that is founded upon cooperating with moderate Muslims is as hopeful as building a skyscraper that is founded upon a cumulous cloud. Both are destined to fail and fall.

I can already hear the rants of the apologists and the pollyannas. "This is an expression of the worst kind of Islamophobia! It is completely unfair to lump all Muslims together and treat them all like rabid jihadists who wantonly torture and murder!" Well, of course it is. No two Muslims are exactly alike. Nor are any two Christians nor Jews nor Buddhists nor Hindus nor goldfish nor bananas. I'm not saying that there are no Muslims who are repulsed by the conduct of the torturers and murderers. What I am saying, to quote a recent Secretary of State, is this: "What difference does it make!?!" What I am saying is that the "moderate Muslim" will never effectively stand against the mainliners, and, therefore, they will never amount to an obstacle to their ambitions. They can't. To oppose the mainliners is to invite being branded as an "apostate" and a "hypocrite" — and that warrants a death sentence in this world and eternal damnation in the next. When push comes to shove, the "moderate Muslim" will join in the shoving while screeching "allahu akbar" at the top of his lungs. Let's explore this a little further.

The apologists and pollyannas will be quick to point out the "moderate" and "peaceful" verses of the *Koran* in order to support their argument that Islam is a religion of peace and that the jihadists are unrepresentative extremists. We've already seen how absurd their conclusion is (namely, that Islam is a religion of peace and that the terrorists are unrepresentative), but let's humor them and consider these "moderate" and "peaceful" verses.

To be sure, the *Koran* offers an assortment of verses ranging from the pacific to the bellicose, sometimes in a strange juxtaposition to one another. For example, in the fifth Sura, "The Table," we read this menacing admonition in verse 33: "This is the recompense of those who fight against God and His Messenger, and hasten about the earth, to do corruption there: they shall be slaughtered, or crucified, or their hands and feet shall alternately be struck off, or they shall be banished from the land. That is a degradation for them in this world; and in the world to come awaits them a mighty chastisement…." Then, in the very next verse, it proclaims, "So know you that God is All-forgiving, All-compassionate" (*Koran*, 5:34). Can you spell "schizophrenic?"

Certainly, there are plenty of kindly and compassionate passages in the *Koran* that Muslim apologists can use to argue for the tolerant and benign nature of their religion. But, how do we reconcile these with the passages calling for chopping off fingers and hands and feet and heads, and crucifixion and slaughter? The answer is "abrogation."

Although the *Koran* is one book, it consists of revelations from two different times with two very different tones. Some of the suras (chapters holding a specific revelation from Allah) were written when Muhammad was still in Mecca. These "Meccan" suras were composed during a time when Muhammad was still trying to woo converts — an effort that was spectacularly unsuccessful. It is in these Meccan suras that we find most of the kinder, gentler verses. However, as we have seen, after Muhammad was chased off to Medina, he adopted a more militaristic manner. Not surprisingly, the divine downloads also became more martial — even savage. These are often referred to as the "Medinan" suras. So, how do we reconcile them?

Once again, Allah conveniently provided Muhammad with a revelation to explain away the apparent contradictions. "And for whatever verse We abrogate or cast into oblivion, We bring a better or the like of it; knowest thou not that God is powerful over everything?" (*Koran*, 2:106) A different translation reads, "None of Our revelations do We abrogate or cause to be forgotten, but We substitute something better or similar: knowest thou not that Allah

Hath power over all things?" So, if we have two contradictory verses from Allah, which one do we use? The principle of "abrogation" says that we use the more recent one. This is why we must not only look at **what** the *Koran* says but **when** the *Koran* said it. And when we do this, we find that most of the kind and compassionate verses are abrogated, or cancelled, by newer, more vicious ones. For example, verse 5 from the ninth sura entitled, "Repentance" or "Immunity", is known as the "Verse of the Sword." It states, "Then, when the sacred months are drawn away, slay the idolaters wherever you find them, and take them, and confine them, and lie in wait for them at every place of ambush. But if they repent, and perform the prayer, and pay the alms, then let them go their way; God is All-forgiving, All-Compassionate." The ninth sura is generally regarded as being the last of the revelations from Allah to Muhammad (remember, the suras are ordered from longest to shortest, not chronologically). Accordingly, this most recent sura abrogates all other verses that contradict its own; and, in fact, the "Verse of the Sword" has been figured to abrogate at least 124 more tolerant and peaceful verses. As many as 225 Koranic verses are overridden or altered by later verses.

Technically speaking, therefore, Muslim apologists are correct when they recite benign and compassionate verses in the *Koran*. They are in there, alright. But what they fail to tell you is that virtually all of them have been abrogated, or canceled, by other, more recent verses. Is this dishonest? Well, at a minimum, it is misleading. It is true that the verses are in the *Koran*, but because of abrogation, this is not what the *Koran* really preaches. So, yes, it is dishonest; but remember, it's okay to lie to Kafirs. You wouldn't be a good Muslim if you didn't.

Now that we have dismissed the myth of the moderate message of the *Koran*, what about "the myth of the moderate Muslim?" Let's see what Islamic doctrine says about them.

To put it simply, Muslims are not allowed to have non-Muslim friends. Their sacred writings as well as the teachings of Muhammad prohibit it. There are roughly a dozen verses in the *Koran* which affirm that Muslims must not befriend Kafirs. Here is a sampling:

"And whosoever takes them for friends, those — they are the evildoers" (*Koran*, 60:9).

"O believers, take not My enemy and your enemy for friends, offering them love, though they have disbelieved in the truth that has come to you, expelling the Messenger and you because you believe in God your Lord. If you go forth to struggle in My way and seek My good pleasure, secretly loving them, yet I know very well what you conceal and what you publish; and whosoever of you does that, has gone astray from the right way" (*Koran*, 60:1). This passage not only prohibits open friendship with Kafirs, it attests that even a secret affection for them will be known by Allah, and we have seen how he handles disloyalty and disobedience.

"O believers, take not Jews and Christians as friends; they are friends of each other. Whoso of you makes them his friends is one of them. God guides not the people of evildoers" (*Koran*, 5:51).

"But," the apologists and pollyannas will protest, "I have Muslims friends!" Are you sure about that? The only thing you can say with certainty is that you know Muslims who **act** friendly — which is exactly what they are expected to do until they achieve a dominant position relative to the Kafirs. "Let not the believers take the unbelievers for friends, rather than the believers — for whoso does that belongs not to God in anything — **unless you have fear of them**" (*Koran*, 3:28, emphasis added). It is permissible for Muslims to act friendly toward Kafirs if it advances the cause of Islam. This is especially true at times when Muslims are in a weak position relative to the Kafirs — when they "have fear of them" — but only until they can turn the tables. Another translation of this verse says, "but you should guard yourselves against them, guarding carefully." The Kafir is always an enemy to be guarded against and, ultimately, to be set up for conversion, slavery, or murder.

"But isn't it unrealistic," the apologists and pollyannas may reply, "to expect all Muslims to follow the same set of rules? After all, not every Christian nor Jew nor Hindu nor Buddhist does that. What if a Muslim has a change of heart and mind? Can't he follow his own path?"

No.

Remember, Islam is not like all the other religions. It is a gang with a god; and one of the characteristics of gangs is that once you are in, it is very difficult — in fact, often fatal — to try to leave. Islam is no different, and the individual Muslim is very aware of that fact. They study the *Koran*. They memorize its verses so thoroughly that they can glibly recite them. That's what the word "Koran" means: recitation. And the *Koran* says, "and whosoever of you turns from his religion, and dies disbelieving — their works have failed in this world and the next; those are the inhabitants of the Fire; therein they shall dwell forever" (*Koran*, 2:217). Even coming to the conclusion that Islam is a false religion and that Allah is a false god will not save you. Allah's nonexistence will spare you from his wrath, but not from the wrath of Muhammad and his remaining followers. The mandate of Muhammad regarding those who leave the faith is still honored with a fearsome vengeance. Muhammad said, "Whoever changed his Islamic religion, then kill him" (Bukhari, 9:88,6922). Muhammad said, "A Muslim who has admitted that there is no god but Allah and that I am His prophet may not be killed except for three reasons: as punishment for murder, for adultery, or for reverting back to non-belief after accepting Islam" (Bukhari, 9,83,17). And again, "the Prophet said, 'If somebody (a Muslim) discards his religion, kill him'" (Bukhari, 4:260).

If you are not a Muslim, they will come after you. If you are a Muslim and try to leave, they will come after you; for it is written, "if they turn their backs, take them, and slay them wherever you find them; take not to yourselves any one of them as friend or helper..." (*Koran*, 4:89).

But what about the Muslims who lament the actions of the terrorists; who say that these monsters are unrepresentative of Islam and have stolen their religion? How do we respond to the Muslims who say they abhor the violence of the "radicals" and merely want to coexist peacefully with the peoples of other religions and cultures? Well, either they are liars — which, as you recall, is perfectly permissible when dealing with Kafirs — or they really aren't Muslims and should start a new religion. Islam was defined fourteen centuries ago by Muhammad's words and deeds, and both his words and deeds command the extermination of the non-Islamic world and the people who inhabit it, either by their submission to Islam or by their violent destruction. To say that one is a Muslim but opposes violence against non-believers is like saying that one is a Christian but opposes the teachings of Christ. Are there people who call themselves Muslims but detest the violence of Islam? Of course, but regardless of what they call themselves, they really are not followers of Islam; and, accordingly, the recommendations to follow do not apply to them.

In summary, then, of course all Muslims are not alike, but they do hold certain things in common. A Muslim is someone who embraces the "Five Pillars of Islam." The most important pillar is the first, "To testify that none has the right to be worshipped but Allah and Muhammad is Allah's Apostle" (Bukhari, 1:7). Allah is what Muhammad said he is. Allah believes what Muhammad said he believes. Allah wants what Muhammad said he wants. And

Muhammad said, "God loveth not the unbelievers" (*Sira*, 406). Muhammad said Muslims are to "slay the idolaters wherever you find them" (*Koran*, 9:5). If you do not believe this, then you are not a Muslim. If you do believe this, then you are no different than the monsters of ISIS, Al Queda, Taliban, Boko Haram, and so forth.

So, are there Muslims with a more moderate disposition than the raving jihadists who torture and burn and behead and bomb? Of course, but as we asked earlier, "What difference does it make?" They will ultimately agree to separate you from your skin in order to keep their own.

CHAPTER SIXTEEN

A BATTLE PLAN

"It is not the function of Islam to compromise with the concepts of Jahiliyyah [the community of non-believers] which are current in the world or to co-exist in the same land together with a jahili system... Islam cannot accept any mixing with Jahiliyyah. Either Islam will remain, or Jahiliyyah; no half-half situation is possible." Muslim Brotherhood theorist and *Koran* commentator Sayyid Qutb in the mid Twentieth Century. ("The Right of Judge", http://www.islamworld.net/justice.html).

Council on American-Islamic Relations (CAIR) chairman Omar Ahmad told a Muslim audience, "Islam isn't in America to be equal to any other faith, but to become dominant. The *Koran* should be the highest authority in America, and Islam the only accepted religion on earth" (Lisa Gardner, "American Muslim Leader Urges Faithful to Spread Islam's Message", San Ramon Valley Herald, July 4, 1998).

"If we had known then what we know now...."

A commonly asked question in ethical discussions since the mid-Twentieth Century goes something like this: "If you had the opportunity to kill Hitler back in 1934, would you?" Okay, reader, you answer the question. Would you be willing to take a single life in order to save roughly 66 million Germans from the tyranny of fascism? Would you be willing to take a single life in order to spare the roughly 10 million people who died in the concentration camps? Would you be willing to take a single life in order to spare humanity the horror of a world war that cost about 40 million civilian and military lives in the European and North African theaters alone?

Here's a different twist on the same ethical question. If the leaders of the free world knew back in 1935 what we know now, would they have been justified in going to war against Nazi Germany even before Hitler's first aggressive move: before reoccupying the Rhineland, before the Anschluss with Austria, before taking the Sudetenland, before seizing the rest of Czechoslovakia, and before overwhelming Poland, vanquishing France, bombing England, marching on North Africa and invading the Soviet Union? By seizing the initiative against nascent Nazism and crushing it in the cradle, we would no longer have been able to save all 50 million of those lives mentioned above (the 40 million from the war and the 10 million in the concentration camps), but we would have been able to save most of them. If you were a national leader back then and you knew what we know now, would you vow to fight Hitler?

Most people would answer with an emphatic "Yes!" to each of these questions. However, we didn't know back then what we know now. Without foreknowledge, it makes a decision to act decisively and violently a much more difficult issue. Back in the early 1930s, we didn't know what Hitler would do. We did know what he said he intended to do, and that alone was pretty menacing; but perhaps he was just blustering for political purposes. Could we justify going to war on the suspicion that he actually meant the outlandish things he said and would follow through on his threats? That is a more difficult question. But that is not the question we face today when we consider the issue of what to do about Islam. We have their words, we have nearly 1,400 years of history, and we have current events — all of which confirm the fact that Islam is a violent, militaristic, aggressive, expansionist, supremacist, intolerant, and totalitarian ideology, theology, and system of government. And unlike Nazi Germany, which had a population of about 66 million in 1934 located almost exclusively in one nation, Islam has a population of over one billion spread around the world. If going to war against Nazi Germany in 1935 would have been both wise and humanitarian, how much more wise and humanitarian would it be to go to war against Islam now? Well, actually, we would not be going to war. We simply would be acknowledging the war that already is raging.

As we prepare to conclude this book — this Primer on Islam — I will offer some thoughts about how the non-Islamic world needs to respond to the current threat posed by Islam. These recommendations will cover the areas of domestic and international policies as well as some anticipated objections to these recommendations. These proposals will be neither moderate nor genteel nor politically correct. That is because the Muslims, themselves, do not allow us such options. They are vicious and relentless and offer us no other alternatives for opposing them and preserving ourselves other than to respond decisively and forcefully. You don't talk a ravenous wolf out of becoming its dinner. You shoot it. So, prepare to lock and load.

Domestic Policy.

It is commonplace — to the point of being trite — for political pundits and commentators to urge people to become "educated" about a problem. Well, of course we should become educated about a problem. But, then what? Unfortunately, the pundits and commentators rarely go beyond the recommendation for illumination. Education is a great start. It is a horrible finish. Education is a means to an and. It is not an end in itself. Education must lead somewhere if it is to have any purpose; so where does our education about Islam lead us? It leads to the conclusion that this is a relentless, aggressive, predatory, and vicious religious-political system that tolerates no opposition and will not stop until it has subjugated the world's population under its hegemony. If you doubt this, just re-read the quotes that opened this chapter. They nicely summarize the information presented in the rest of this book. So, assuming that we are not willing to convert, be enslaved, or killed, what are our options?

In the face of such a relentless and ravenous foe, our only domestic options are assimilation, annihilation, or deportation. Let us briefly consider each.

Assimilation is not an option because the Muslims will not do it. Remember, they, themselves, have ruled out co-existence. In their playbook it is "us or them." Accordingly, they will never simply blend into our culture and adopt a policy of "live-and-let-live," like Hindus or Buddhists or Shintos or atheists. Our national and cultural bodies can assimilate them no better than our physical bodies can assimilate cyanide. Once they have insinuated them-selves into a culture, their goal is not to assimilate and participate. It is to devastate and dominate.

Next, whereas our goal must be to annihilate Islam — because it **is** quite literally us or them — our goal should not be to annihilate Muslims. Our objective should be to liberate them from the bondage of the oppressive and dehumanizing Islamic system. This, however, will take a substantial commitment of time and other resources. In the meanwhile, we cannot allow Islam to continue to penetrate and subvert our various nations and cultures. Islam is a social disease, and each Muslim is like a cancer cell, threatening the very survival of our national, reli-gious, and cultural identities.

This leaves but one alternative for the short-to-intermediate term: deportation. We must insist that Muslims either (1) truly renounce their religion and abandon its principles or (2) leave. Then we must enforce this policy. A cancer patient cannot tolerate the uncontrolled presence of cancer cells within his body. They will eventually metastasize and kill him. The same is true of Muslims within a national body.

We must anticipate a hostile reaction to this policy from the Muslims and their sympathizers. Protests will erupt and acts of terrorism will likely increase. Accordingly, we must take measures to enhance intelligence gathering and security in order to minimize the consequences of this hostile reaction. The problem from native Muslims will diminish as the deportation proceeds, for there will be fewer and fewer of them. However, the danger from foreign jihadists will increase. For this, and for other reasons, we must work to seal our borders in order to better control clandestine entry into the nation. We have known for years that foreign terrorists have been cultivating a relationship with Mexican drug cartels because of the pathways they already have paved into the United States. This should have been addressed long ago, but the corruption associated with the politics of immigration have thwarted a remedy. We can no longer afford to play this game. We must close and secure the borders.

It also is important to point out that this increase in violence will not be the product of this policy of deportation. The violence is coming. By dealing with the danger decisively now, we will see a little more violence in the short-term and a lot less violence in the long-term. It is an acceptable trade-off. In fact, to do otherwise would be worse than foolhardy — it would be criminal, even traitorous.

I can already smell the fumes wafting from the outraged Islamic apologists, pollyannas, and misguided civil rights activists who are burning with righteous indignation. "This is America! We have rights, including religious freedom. And those rights extend even to those with whom we disagree — especially to those with whom we disagree." Of course they have rights, but those rights do not extend to people who would use their liberties to deny and destroy the rights of others. They never have. No responsible theory of rights has ever presumed to allow a completely unrestrained exercise of those rights. May I kill someone and justify it on religious grounds by claiming that my faith believes in human sacrifices? Of course not. May I have two wives and justify it on religious grounds by claiming that my faith believes in polygamy? No. In fact, that very issue was addressed back in 1878 by the United States Supreme Court in *Reynolds v. United States* where the Court ruled unanimously that a law banning polygamy was constitutional and did not infringe upon an individual's First Amendment right to religious freedom. Does my right to free speech allow me to shout "Fire!" in a crowded theater, thereby inducing a panic when there is no fire? No. Justice Oliver Wendell Holmes, Jr. stated as much in *Schenck v. United States* in 1919.

There are limits to the exercise of our rights, and the boundary is usually drawn at the point where the exercise of one party's rights infringes on the opportunity of another party to exercise his rights; and this is exactly what Muslims do. Remember, "convert, be enslaved, or die" is the official policy of Islam toward Kafirs; and this policy certainly "infringes on the opportunity of another to exercise his rights." By definition, Islam places itself outside the boundary of protected rights.

Secondly, we are at war with Islam — a war they declared. The Muslims have understood this for nearly fourteen centuries. It is high time for the rest of the world to acknowledge that this state of war exists and act accordingly. This is relevant to our current discussion of rights because a declaration of war changes the legal status of belligerents. Specifically, enemy agents are not afforded the same protections as others. American Nazis were generally allowed to speak their minds until December 11, 1941. On that day, the United States declared war on the Third Reich, and Nazi sympathizers instantly became enemy agents. The same speech that was protected the day before could lead to arrest and incarceration a day later.

The evidence leads us to an inescapable conclusion. There can be no coexistence with Islam. All Muslims are commanded by their god and prophet to wage relentless jihad against the Kafirs. This can be done as blatantly as military invasions, beheadings, bombings, and other terrorist activities, or as subtly as funding Islamic study programs, perpetuating the lie that Islam is a religion of peace, or smiling and waving at neighbors as they drive by. The objective is always the same. The Kafir must be converted, enslaved, or killed. So, unless our choice is to be converted, enslaved, or killed, we must join the fight. Individual Muslims in our nations are enemy agents and need to be treated as such. We, however, can deal with the danger they pose by offering them more compassionate alternatives than they offer us; namely, renounce and abandon their religion or leave. If they are unhappy with Islam, here is a golden opportunity to escape. If they are happy with Islam, then go to an Islamic nation. We, however, do not wish to become Islamic, and we intend to keep it that way.

International Policy.

The danger of Islam is not just intranational, it is international as well; and, so, we must devise a global response to this threat. Islam has pursued an unrelenting and ruthless policy of international aggression since the seventh century. Merely purging our nations and cultures of Muslims will do nothing to end the long-term threat. There must be a deliberate, concerted, and coordinated plan implemented by an alliance of non-Islamic nations in order to save themselves by eliminating Islam. Here's how.

Any good military commander, fire fighter, or oncologist will tell you that the first objective in dealing with an aggressive enemy is to contain the threat. Accordingly, once we have deported the Muslims from our own nations and deposited them in other, Islamic countries, we next must quarantine these nations in order to prevent renewed expansion. In effect, we turn these Islamic countries into national penitentiaries and insure that their personnel, products, and ideologies do not escape.

Containment, however, is not likely to accomplish much nor last long unless we follow up immediately with measures to weaken and attrit the enemy. This should be pursued in a variety of ways including politically, economically, culturally, and militarily. For example, politically, we expel Islamic nations from alliances and associations involving non-Islamic countries. We must ensure that they have no say, they have no vote, and they have no influence outside the Islamic penitentiary. Economically, we neither buy their goods nor sell to them. In addition to this, there are a variety of other economic measures available for us to cripple them and their ability to fund jihad. Included among these are freezing and seizing assets, quarantines, and embargoes. Islamic nations and cultures have been among the most unproductive societies in history. To be sure, their apologists will point to a variety of innovations which have been spawned by the Islamic empire; but upon closer inspection we see that virtually all of these, including Arabic numbers, were created by or stolen from conquered peoples. Islam is barren, and if we dam the flow of commerce with it, it will starve to death. Similarly, we hamstring its noxious cultural impact by reducing its propaganda efforts, which are carried out largely through the various "Islamic Study Programs" at our colleges and elsewhere, and through the work of Islamic embassies and sympathetic organizations around the world.

Ultimately, however, there will most likely need to be a military solution. History and personal experience all confirm the fact that force is the ultimate arbiter. Love, reason, and money may sway human behavior from time to time, but force trumps them all. The history of Islam is a telling witness to this. Muhammad, himself, was spectacularly unsuccessful for over thirteen years until he resorted to force. It was then that his shabby band of Muslims began to grow and, ultimately, to establish a huge empire — by force. It truly is a shame that this is the way the world is, but this is the way the world is, and pretending it isn't won't change that. It merely defines whom the next victims will be. We always can choose not to use force, but if we choose not to have force, we ensure that we ultimately will become the victims of those who did not abjure its use. Islam will "not go gentle into that good night." It will need to be forced into the abyss.

Accordingly, we need to prepare to unleash the martial option. We need to build and train a formidable military force. Simultaneously, we must thwart the development of additional military might by Islamic nations. Among other things, it should be obvious to anyone who is neither microcephalic nor a conscious traitor to his nation that Islamic countries must be denied the development and possession of weapons of mass destruction.

Included in this are nuclear, biological, and chemical weaponry.

Once our military option is credible and ready to deploy, we need to initiate action to establish a firm beachhead and prepare for follow-on actions. More specifically, we should make it our committed objective to establish a territorially large Israeli nation that is geographically, economically, and militarily secure. Politically, Israel is our best ally in the region. It, also, is a specific target of Islam. We must protect it for their sake and for our own. Geographically, the eastern Mediterranean region is strategically critical, in that it forms a land bridge linking three continents. A secure and friendly Israel is essential to our future. Coordinated efforts with Israel will establish our beachhead and form a mighty bastion and base for subsequent operations.

Next, we need to create large, geographically, economically, politically, and militarily secure neighbors and allies around Israel under Christian administration. This will secure our Israeli ally, enlarge our base of operation, deny critical areas and their resources to the Islamic enemy, and provide a much-needed safe haven for Christians and other civilized populations in the region.

While this is taking place, we must conduct a masterfully crafted, well-funded, and skillfully executed plan to destabilize the ruling class in Islamic nations. We should provide resources to indigenous opposition groups, so they can wage the battle from within. Simultaneously, we inform the masses of the coming wrath **if** they do not depose and dispose of the Islamists themselves. From the time of Muhammad's death to the recent secular uprisings in Iran, we have witnessed strong evidence of the popular hatred for Islam. Many want to be free of it, but the leadership is too powerful and ruthless to oppose — at least under the current conditions. We need to change those conditions and provide committed and consistent support for those who seek to be liberated from the horror of Islam. Our military preparations will give them all the more confidence to revolt — and in the end, we may not need to fire a shot. The discontented, once liberated, could seize power within these Islamic nations and finish the job of annihilating Islam themselves.

Ah, but once again, we can hear the mournful wailing of the self-proclaimed "Voices of Reason." Incredulity paints their faces while their voices drip with derision. "You've got to be kidding! We've tried violence, and what has it accomplished? Do you have any idea how much your proposal will cost in money and lives?"

No, I am not kidding. Yes, we have tried violence, but we haven't tried winning — at least not in this context. Every time the United States has tried to win, we have done so while achieving remarkable results. We won the American Revolution. We won the War of 1812. We won the Barbary Wars. We won the Mexican-American War. We won the Civil War. We won the Spanish-American War. We won World War I. We won World War II. We won the Korean War — sort of. But from that time on, other objectives have crowded out victory, and all we have done is waste trillions of dollars and tens of thousands of lives. And this, of course, leads to that last question: "Do you have any idea how much your proposal will cost in money and lives?" No, not exactly, but I do know this: Whatever this course of action will cost will be substantially less than if we fail to fight and destroy the enemy now. And that settles the matter, doesn't it? And let me repeat: if we successfully fan the flames of anti-Islamic sentiment within the Islamic countries themselves, we may not have to go to war at all. However, I am always ready to concede the possibility that I may be wrong. So, if you have a better way of dealing with the ravenous wolf that is bearing down on you than to shoot it, I'm all ears. But if you don't, then I strongly suggest that you get behind me, because all your olive branch will do is add a little seasoning to the wolf's meal.

Finally, a word to the ideologically fashionable and politically correct simpletons who will try to dismiss me as a "Hater." I confess, this is about hate; but not my hate for Muslims. It is about their hate for us. Remember, "you [Muslims] have more right to hate them [the Kafirs] than they to hate you" (*Sira*, 388). It is a hate which they have relentlessly and savagely stoked for nearly fourteen hundred years. It is a hate which has tortured millions, killed tens of millions, enslaved tens of millions more, and oppressed hundreds of millions. It is about the worst case of systematic hatred in human history. It is about Islam. It is about the world war that Muhammad initiated fourteen centuries ago. It is about a war that continues to be waged against all Kafirs. I didn't start this war, but I have no intention of denying it; and I certainly have no intention of losing it.

I don't hate Muslims. I feel horribly about their enslavement and brutalization. They are shackled by the chains of a stifling, abusive, ritualistic religion and held in bondage by fear. I don't hate them. I long for their liberation. If you have an ounce of compassion within you, you must feel the same way. They are victims, and we can save them. They can be manumitted from their slavery. They can be liberated from their bondage. They can be rescued from the oppression that Allah and Muhammad have imposed upon them. But they are going to need some help.

During World War II, my dad rose to the challenge of his age and chose to risk everything in order to stop a vicious, totalitarian system that had enslaved millions and would kill millions more. He piloted B-24 bombers over Europe. The name given to that warplane was "Liberator." The challenge of this age, once again, is to risk everything in order to stop a vicious, totalitarian system that has enslaved tens of millions and has killed tens of millions more. Once again, we need a Liberator. I have resolved to fight this war of liberation. I have resolved to perform this labor of love and free over a billion people from their bondage — whatever the cost. What have you resolved to do?

KEY VERSES

Abrogation:

"And for whatever verse We abrogate or cast into oblivion, We bring a better or the like of it; knowest thou not that God is powerful over everything?" (*Koran*, 2:106) A different translation reads, "None of Our revelations do We abrogate or cause to be forgotten, but We substitute something better or similar: knowest thou not that Allah Hath power over all things?"

Allah the Terrorist:

"When your Lord revealed to the angels: I am with you, therefore make firm those who believe. I will cast terror into the hearts of those who disbelieve. Therefore strike off their heads and strike off every fingertip of them" (*Koran*, 8:12).

Christians:

"They are unbelievers who say, 'God is the Messiah, Mary's son'" (*Koran*, 5:17).

"God has not taken to Himself any son…" (*Koran*, 23:91).

"It is not for God to take a son unto Him" (*Koran*, 19:35).

Muhammad said, "You lie. Your assertion that God has a son, your worship of the cross, and your eating pork hold you back from submission" (*Sira*, 403).

"They are unbelievers who say, 'God is the Messiah, Mary's son.' For the Messiah said, 'Children of Israel, serve Allah, my Lord and your Lord. Verily whoso associates with God anything, God shall prohibit him entrance to Paradise, and his refuge shall be the Fire; and wrongdoers shall have no helpers.' They are unbelievers who say, 'God is the Third of Three.' No god is there but One God" (*Koran*, 5:72-73).

"And when Jesus son of Mary said, 'Children of Israel, I am indeed the Messenger of God to you, confirming the Torah that is before me, and giving good tidings of a Messenger who shall come after me, whose name shall be Ahmad'" (*Koran*, 61:6). "Ahmad" means "highly praised" and has the same root as "Muhammad."

Coexistence is not an Option:

'I will cast terror into the hearts of those who disbelieve, so strike off their heads and cut off all their fingers, because they opposed God and His apostle and he who opposes God and His apostle, (will find) God severe in punishment" (*Sira*, 477). This quotation from *Sirat Rasul Allah* essentially reiterates verses from the eighth "Sura" of the *Koran*: "When thy Lord was revealing to the angels, 'I am with you; so confirm the believers. I shall cast into the unbelievers' hearts terror; so smite above the necks, and smite every finger of them!' That, because they had made a breach with God and with his Messenger; and whosoever makes a breach with God and with His Messenger, surely God is terrible in retribution" (*Koran* 8:12-14).

"It is not the function of Islam to compromise with the concepts of Jahiliyyah [the community of non-believers] which are current in the world or to co-exist in the same land together with a jahili system…. Islam cannot accept any mixing with Jahiliyyah. Either Islam will remain, or Jahiliyyah; no half-half situation is possible." Muslim Brotherhood theorist and *Koran* commentator Sayyid Qutb in the mid Twentieth Century. ("The Right of Judge," http://www.islamworld.net/justice.html)

Council on American-Islamic Relations (CAIR) chairman Omar Ahmad told a Muslim audience, "Islam isn't in America to be equal to any other faith, but to become dominant. The *Koran* should be the highest authority in America, and Islam the only accepted religion on earth." (Lisa Gardner, "American Muslim Leader Urges Faithful to Spread Islam's Message," San Ramon Valley Herald, July 4, 1998.)

Death Glorified:

Muhammad said, "By Him in Whose Hands my life is! I would love to be martyred in Allah's Cause and then get resurrected and then get martyred, and then get resurrected again and then get martyred and then get resurrected again and then get martyred" (Bukhari, 4:54).

"The Prophet said, 'Nobody who enters Paradise likes to go back to the world even if he got everything on the earth, except a Mujahid [holy warrior] who wishes to return to the world so that he may be martyred ten times because of the dignity he receives (from Allah)'" (Bukhari, 4:72).

Friends:

"And whosoever takes them [Karirs] for friends, those — they are the evildoers" (*Koran*, 60:9).

"Let not the believers take the unbelievers [Kafirs] for friends, rather than the believers — for whoso does that belongs not to God in anything" (*Koran*, 3:28).

"O believers, take not My enemy and your enemy for friends, offering them love, though they have disbelieved in the truth that has come to you, expelling the Messenger and you because you believe in God your Lord. If you go forth to struggle in My way and seek My good pleasure, secretly loving them, yet I know very well what you conceal and what you publish; and whosoever of you does that, has gone astray from the right way" (*Koran*, 60:1).

"'O you who believe, do not choose those outside our community as intimate friends. They will spare no pains to corrupt you longing for your ruin'... you have more right to hate them than they to hate you" (*Sira*, 388).

Intolerance:
"God loveth not the unbelievers" (*Sira*, 406).

"[F]ight everyone in the way of God and kill those who disbelieve in God" (*Sira*, 992).

"When your Lord revealed to the angels: I am with you, therefore make firm those who believe. I will cast terror into the hearts of those who disbelieve. Therefore strike off their heads and strike off every fingertip of them" (*Koran*, 8:12).

"When you meet the unbelievers, smite their necks [cut off their heads], then, when you have made wide slaughter among them, tie fast the bonds; then set them free, either by grace or ransom, till the war lays down its loads" (*Koran*, 47:4).

Jews:
"But God has cursed them for their unbelief and only a few will believe" (*Sira*, 390) (*Koran*, 4:46).

"Allah's Apostle said, 'May Allah curse the Jews... (Bukhari, 3:427).

"The apostle said, 'Kill any Jew that falls into your power.' (*Sira*, 554).

"Allah's Apostle said, 'You (i.e. Muslims) will fight with the Jews till some of them will hide behind stones. The stones will (betray them) saying, "O Abdullah (i.e. slave of Allah)! There is a Jew hiding behind me; so kill him"'" (Bukhari, 4:176).

Muhammad said, "A tribe of Jews disappeared. I do not know what became of them, but I think they changed and became rats" (Muslim, 042,7135).

Jihad:

"Allah's Apostle said: 'I have been ordered (by Allah) to fight against the people until they testify that none has the right to be worshipped but Allah and that Muhammad is Allah's Apostle...'" (Bukhari, 1:24).

"Allah's Apostle was asked, 'What is the best deed?' He replied, 'To believe in Allah and His Apostle (Muhammad).' The questioner then asked, 'What is the next (in goodness)?' He replied, 'To participate in Jihad (religious fighting) in Allah's Cause.'" (Bukhari, 4:50).

Muhammad said, "Two angels descend from Paradise each day. One says, 'O, Allah! Reward those who contribute

to jihad,' and the other says, 'O, Allah! Kill those who refuse to support jihad'" (Bukhari, 2,24,522).

Muhammad said, "Allah promises that anyone killed
while fighting for His cause will be admitted without
question into Paradise. If such a holy warrior survives
the battles, he can return home with the captured
property and possessions of the defeated" (Bukhari,
4:52,46).

"Muhammad   cried   out,   'Jihad   is   deceit'"
(Bukhari,4:52,267).

No Safe Escape:

Muhammad said, "Whoever changed his Islamic religion, then kill him" (Bukhari, 9:88,6922).

Muhammad said, "A Muslim who has admitted that
there is no god but Allah and that I am His prophet may
not be killed except for three reasons: as punishment for
murder, for adultery, or for reverting back to non-belief
after accepting Islam" (Bukhari, 9,83,17).

"[T]he Prophet said, 'If somebody (a Muslim) discards
his religion, kill him'" (Bukhari, 4:260).

"[I]f they turn their backs, take them, and slay them
wherever you find them; take not to yourselves any one
of them as friend or helper…" (Koran, 4:89).

OTHER TENETS OF ISLAM

Abortion.

A follower once asked Muhammad, "'O Allah's Apostle! We get female captives as our share of booty, and we are interested in their prices, what is your opinion about coitus interruptus?' The Prophet said, 'Do you really do that? It is better for you not to do it. No soul that which Allah has destined to exist, but will surely come into existence'" (Bukhari, 3:432). Clarification: Captured women were treated as booty. Muslim men wanted to enjoy their favors but not reduce their sale price by getting them pregnant, so they practiced coitus interruptus. Muhammad didn't object to how they treated women, but he told them they shouldn't practice coitus interruptus because every soul intended by Allah should be born. Implications for abortion.

"That he heard the Prophet delivering a sermon on the pulpit saying, 'Kill snakes and kill Dhu-at-Tufyatain (i.e.

a snake with two white lines on its back) and ALBATROSS (i.e. a snake with short or mutilated tail) for they destroy the sight of one's eyes and bring about abortion'" (Bukhari, 4:518).

Abraham's Religion.

"No; Abraham in truth was not a Jew, neither a Christian; but he was a Muslim and one of pure faith…" (*Koran*, 3:67).

Astronomy.

"The Prophet asked me at sunset, 'Do you know where the sun goes (at the time of sunset)?' I replied 'Allah and His Apostle know better.' He said, 'It goes (i.e. travels) till it prostrates itself underneath the Throne and takes the permission to rise again…" (Bukhari, 4:421).

Borrowing and Begging.

"And an upper (i.e. giving) hand is better than a lower (i.e. taking) hand…" (Bukhari, 4:371).

"[T]he best among you are those who repay their debts handsomely" (Bukhari, 3:575).

"The Prophet said, "Allah has forbidden for you, (1) to be undutiful to your mothers, (2) to bury your daughters alive, (3) to not pay the rights of the others (e.g. charity, etc.) and (4) to beg of men (begging)" (Bukhari, 3:591).

Diseases and cures.

"The Prophet said 'If a house fly falls in the drink of anyone of you, he should dip it (in the drink), for one of its wings has a disease and the other has the cure for the disease'" (Bukhari,4:537).

Dogs.

"Allah's Apostle said, 'Whoever keeps a dog, one Qirat of the reward of his good deeds is deducted daily, unless the dog is used for guarding a farm or cattle" (Bukhari 3:515).

"Abu Sufyan bin Abu Zuhair, a man from Azd Shanua and one of the companions of the Prophet said, 'I heard Allah's Apostle saying, "if one keeps a dog which is meant for guarding neither farm nor cattle, one Qirat of the reward of his good deeds is deducted daily." I said, "Did you hear this from Allah's Apostle?" He said, "Yes, by the Lord of this Mosque"'" (Bukhari, 3:516).

"I heard Alah's Apostle saying; "Angels (of Mercy) do not enter a house wherein there is a dog or a picture of a living creature (a human being or an animal)'" (Bukhari, 4:448).

"Once Gabriel promised the Prophet (that he would visit him, but Gabriel did not come) and later on he said, 'We angels, do not enter a house which contains a picture or a dog'" (Bukhari, 4:450).

"Allah's Apostle ordered that the dogs should be killed" (Bukhari, 4:540).

Dreams.

"The Prophet said, 'A good dream is from Allah, and a bad or evil dream is from Satan; so if anyone of you has a bad dream of which he gets afraid, he should spit on his left side and should seek Refuge with Allah from its evil, for then it will not harm him'" (Bukhari, 4:513).

Homosexuality.

"What, do you come to male beings, leaving your wives that your Lord created for you? Nay, but you are a people of transgressors… So We delivered him [Lot] and his people all together, save an old woman among those that tarried; then We destroyed the others…" (*Koran*, 26:165-6,170-2).

"And Lot, when he said to his people, 'What, do you commit indecency with your eyes open? What, do you approach men lustfully instead of women? No, you are a people that are ignorant" (*Koran*, 27:55).

"And Lot, when he said to his people 'Surely you commit such indecency as never any being in all the world committed before you. What, do you approach men, and cut the way, and commit in your assembly dishonor?… 'My Lord, help me against the people what work corruption.' And when Our messengers came to

Abraham with the good tidings, they said, 'We shall destroy the people of this city, for its people are evildoers.'... 'We shall send down upon then people of this city wrath out of heaven for their ungodliness'" (*Koran*, 29:28-31,34).

"The Prophet said, "Kill the one who sodomizes and the one who lets it be done to him" (Umdat al-Salik, p.17.3 (1) Umdat al-Salik, or *The Reliance of the Traveller*, was composed in the 14th Century and is an authoritative summation of Islamic jurisprudence).

Intoxicants.

"The Prophet said, 'All drinks that produce intoxication are Haram (forbidden to drink)'" (Bukhari, 1:243).

"When the last verses of Surat-al-Baqara were revealed, the Prophet went out (of his house to the Mosque) and said, 'The trade of alcohol has become illegal'" (Bukhari, 3:429).

"Once Umar was informed that a certain man sold alcohol. Umar said, 'May Allah curse him!'" (Bukhari, 3:426).

"When An-Nuaman or his son was brought in a state of drunkenness, Allah's Apostle ordered all those who were present in the house to beat him. I was was one of those who beat him. We beat him with shoes and palm-leaf stalks" (Bukhari, 3:509).

Pictures.

Muhammad said, "Don't you know that angels do not enter a house wherein there are pictures; and whoever makes a picture will be punished on the Day of Resurrection and will be asked to give life to (what he has created)?" (Bukhari, 4:447).

"I heard Alah's Apostle saying; "Angels (of Mercy) do not enter a house wherein there is a dog or a picture of a living creature (a human being or an animal)'" (Bukhari, 4:448).

"Once Gabriel promised the Prophet (that he would visit him, but Gabriel did not come) and later on he said, 'We angels, do not enter a house which contains a picture or a dog'" (Bukhari, 4:450).

Predestination.

"Allah's Apostle, the true and truly inspired said, '(The matter of the Creation of) a human being is put together in the womb of the mother in forty days, and then he becomes a clot of thick blood for a similar period, and then a piece of flesh for a similar period. Then Allah sends an angel who is ordered to write four things. He is ordered to write down his (i.e. the new creature's) deeds, his livelihood, his (date of) death, and whether he will be blessed or wretched (in religion). Then the soul is breathed into him. So, a man amongst you may do (good deeds till there is only a cubit between him and Paradise and then what has been written for him decides his behavior and he starts doing (evil) deeds characteristic of the people of the (Hell) fire. And similarly a man amongst you may do (evil) deeds till there is only a cubit between him and the (Hell) Fire, and then what has been written for him decides his behavior, and he starts doing deeds characteristic of the people of Paradise'" (Bukhari, 4:430).

"Allah's Apostle said, 'Adam and Moses argued with each other. Moses said to Adam, "You are Adam whose mistake expelled you from Paradise." Adam said to him, "You are Moses whom Allah selected as His Messenger and as the one to whom He spoke directly, yet you blame me for a thing which had already been written in my fate before my creation?"' Allah's Apostle said twice, 'So Adam overpowered Moses'" (Bukhari, 4:621).

Protecting Your Children from the Devil.

"The Prophet said, 'If anyone of you, when having sexual relations with his wife, say "In the name of Allah. O Allah! Protect us from Satan and prevent Satan from approaching our offspring you are going to give us,' and if he begets a child (as a result of that relation) Satan will not harm it." I suppose it beats talking dirty.

Rank Order of Importance of Scriptural Personalities.

Muhammad gives an account of a vision he had where he met personalities at the various levels of heaven. The higher the level the better.

First level (lowest): Adam

Second level: Jesus and John

Third level: Joseph, son of Israel

Fourth level: Idris, an early Islamic prophet

Fifth level: Aaron

Sixth level: Moses

Seventh level (highest): Abraham

Satan.

"The Prophet said, 'If anyone of you rouses from sleep and performs the ablution [ritual cleansing], he should wash his nose by putting water in it and then blowing it out thrice, because Satan has stayed in the upper part of his nose all the night'" (Bukhari, 4:517).

"The Prophet said, 'When you hear the crowing of cocks, ask for Allah's Blessings for (their crowing indicates that) they have seen an angel. And when you hear the braying of donkeys, seek Refuge with Allah from Satan for (their braying indicates) that they have seen a Satan" (Bukhari, 4:522).

Yawning.

"The Prophet said, 'Yawning is from Satan and if anyone of you yawns, he should check his yawning as much as possible, for if anyone of you (during the act of yawning) should say: "Ha", Satan will laugh at him'" (Bukhari, 4:509).

The Islamic List of Top Ten Unclean (najis) Things.

10. The sweat of an animal that persistently eats unclean things.

9. Alcoholic liquors.

8. Kafirs (non-believers, infidels)

7. Pig

6. Dog

5. Blood

4. Dead body

3. Semen

2. Feces

And the Number One unclean thing: Urine

This list was created by Iran"s Grand Ayatollah Sayyid Ali Husayni Sistani who has been praised by some in the West as a moderate and reformer. (http://quod.lib.umich.edu/k/koran/browse.html).

Meaningful Bureaucratic, Regulatory, and Budget Reform

Redefining Citizenship and Voter Rights

The Truth About Separation of Church and State

The Liberation of Theology: Debunking the Myths that Keep Christians Out of the Fight and in Chains

Winning for God by Changing the Spiritual Energy in America

Call (909) 913-7878 to schedule an event with Mr. Hebron or to get a quote for volume discounts and shipping costs on his books.

Made in the USA
Middletown, DE
21 May 2017